Grieving:
My Pilgrimage of Love

Engaging Grief for Healing and Hope

By Gary L. Crawford, D.Min.

"Blessed are those . . . who have set their heart on pilgrimage."
Psalm 84:5

BRIDGE
LOGOS

Alachua, Florida 32615
Christian Living | Grief Consolation

Bridge-Logos

Alachua, FL 32615 USA

International Standard Book Number: 978-088270860-7
Library of Congress Control Number: 2012940604

Unless otherwise indicated, Bible quotations are taken from the New International Version of the Bible, copyright © 1973, 1978, 1984 by International Bible Society. Published by Zondervan Publishing House.

Bible quotations marked KJV are from the King James Version.

About the Author

Gary Crawford has served as Senior Pastor of Westside Baptist Church in Gainesville, Florida for thirty-one years. He holds degrees in science, theology, and leadership. He is a gifted communicator, author, teacher, and leader. He has served in multiple leadership positions in various organizations nationally and internationally, leading both non-profits and businesses in organizational design and transitions, strategy planning, problem solving, and leadership development.

His heart is for family, ministry, and missions, as well as leadership development.

He was married to the late Freda Mangle Crawford for thirty-nine years. He lives in Gainesville, as do his two children with their spouses and his six grandchildren.

Endorsements

Having suffered the loss of my wife of thirty years after a long battle with cancer, I sought the counsel of my pastor, Gary Crawford. I needed to speak with someone who could relate to my situation. Since Pastor Gary had lost his wife Freda, also following a battle with cancer, I felt comfortable discussing my grief with him. As a twenty-five-year veteran of the FBI, I have been involved in numerous arrest scenarios. I have witnessed the deaths of fellow agents, as well as violent criminals who were the subjects of federal arrest warrants. Due to the nature of the job, I have been conditioned to place the mission above personal emotions. The most beneficial aspect of my contact with Pastor Gary was being afforded the opportunity to read this book. In reading the book, I fit the description of the typical male described therein. My inability to express my emotions and speak freely to other men about my situation was crippling. The book freed me to express my grief and gave me the confidence to speak to other men about my personal experience. I am confident that you will find this book liberating and helpful in your journey through grief. **— Steve Amos, FBI Agent**

I will unashamedly admit that I wept through so much of this book of love. At times I felt as if I were observing a very sacred intimacy between a man and woman. Pastor Gary seemingly has the ability to open his heart wide and, without embarrassment, to invite all to come in, walk around, and experience with him the joy of such a woman as his beloved Freda. I have never personally heard a man give such honor to his wife, except for my own beloved. I applaud Pastor Gary that there was no emotion he was not willing to express in order to share the depth of his love and gratitude for this love of his youth. I have no doubt many will read it and feel such a bond with him that only those who have lost such a love can experience. I am better for having read it. **— Cheryl Carter, Team Pastor of The Rock of Gainesville, Florida**

I have just had the very moving experience of reading Pastor Gary's book on grief. I felt I was there with him, experiencing his revisiting of places and people. Here are a few responses:

- The book is introspective and very personal and intimate.
- The vocabulary is wonderful and the writing style smooth.
- Pastor Gary has made and kept many great friends along the way and has a great staff and church family who love him and support him in his absences and his grieving.
- The list of "Insights from Grief" is a great result/summary of his experiences and journeys.
- While I never got to meet Freda, I feel like I know her and that she would be most proud of Pastor Gary and this work.
- I congratulate and thank Pastor Gary for letting me read this special story and learn more about his life with Freda.

— **Dr. Charles Hall, President, Florida Gateway College**

Grieving: My Pilgrimage of Love is not the typical "how to deal with grief" book that offers some platitudes and pithy principles of coping with the devastation of the death of a loved one. This intensely personal journal of Pastor Gary is a glimpse into the soul of a Christian who "walks in the valley of the shadow of death" and comes through the valley to tell his story. It's a love story that is real: love that isn't perfect and love that sometimes hurts, but it's love because it's about the faithfulness of a wife and her husband through the good times of living and the horrible times of dying. Pastor Gary's message is immensely personal and descriptive. It will give insight to the inner thoughts of a true Christian believer who struggles with the pain and separation he endures after having thirty-nine years with his beloved Freda. Readers will take comfort in that followers of Jesus aren't immune to grief but, if anything, are touched more deeply by it. Yet the book encourages because the end result is that there is meaning to life—all of it. The best and the worst of it are part of *Grieving: My Pilgrimage of Love.*

— **Governor Mike Huckabee**

In *Grieving: My Pilgrimage of Love* Pastor Gary is transparent about his grief and the journey he has taken to find life after the loss of his wife. As one who has also been on that journey after the loss of my husband, I found great comfort in his insightfulness. His book challenged me to embrace grief and not shy away from it. For me grieving had become a process of "surviving." Through this book, I was encouraged to become intentional. I addressed things I thought would be too painful. I found even through the heartache and tears, that by facing those things, healing was in the process. It is a process that continues, but I am finding freedom in the anticipation to accomplish the purpose God has for my life. For anyone who has lost a loved one, I would highly recommend this book to aid the grieving process.
— Diane Junior, Personal friend

Loss is a part of life. We will all experience loss in some form, be it through death, divorce, rejection, or abandonment. And loss is painful and requires us to grieve that loss. Grieving is a normal response to loss, and *how* we grieve is what matters. Some find the pain of loss too great and rationalize, move into denial, get stuck in anger and bitterness, while others face the pain of grief and take the journey through it to find health and healing. Pastor Gary's story is one of courage to face one of life's greatest losses and the hope and healing that comes through walking that grief journey with the love and compassion of Abba and family and friends.

As I read through this story, both times I found myself with tears in my eyes. I found myself relating to his story of loss and his journey through the healing. I found myself joyful for him for the love and life he shared with his precious wife and friend of so many wonderful years. But what I found mostly was his courage, his transparency, his honesty, and his devotion not only to his God, wife, family, and friends, but also to you and me. For in this book he shares not just information, but his feelings, thoughts, pains, and joys. The reader going through his or her own journey can relate to Pastor Gary's journey and, yet, is left with a path for healing and most importantly, hope. And Pastor Gary makes it clear that this hope comes in a relationship with Abba God. He helps us understand that we can celebrate the good things of the past and realize that we can celebrate life in the future. As I read through this journey, I found myself walking it with him. Feeling his hopes, and learning from his insights make this book more of a testimony to healing rather than a book on grief.

I think this book will be a leading book on understanding the pain of loss and how we can be courageous to face the loss, the pain, the emptiness, the hole left in our hearts and how Christ fills the loss with purpose and meaning for a life into the future. Pastor Gary does not give us a "pie in the sky" understanding of healing, but with great humility and transparency, lets us walk his journey of healing and in the midst of walking his journey with him, we can allow ourselves to embrace our own journey. Pastor Gary provides us a map for how this can be accomplished. I hope you find this journey of one man's loss and love for wife and family just as inspiring as I did. I must admit, I gained a deeper appreciation for my wife and children once having read through this work.
—Richard Marks, Ph.D, Marriage and Family Counseling

Grieving: My Pilgrimage of Love teaches us a great deal about facing grief, using it for personal growth and coming to terms with it by accepting it as a natural response to loss. But above all, Pastor Gary's courageous battle with grief shows us that the pain of loss can be shared with others, and in the process a loving memory becomes a means to outlast time.
—Shelley Fraser Mickle, Novelist and Radio Commentator

Pastor Gary has done a wonderful service in letting others have a window into his soul. It was a selfless decision to let others benefit from the most painful experience of his life. Pastor Gary and Freda were blessed with a special marriage, and their journey is captured well through Pastor Gary's words. Healing is helped through being honest with ourselves. Pastor Gary's honest evaluation of life with and without Freda has helped him and, more importantly, will help countless others in their healing. **—Mike Nichols, Personal friend**

In a day of "cheerleader" Christianity, I thank the Lord for the service Pastor Gary has provided for the Body of Christ. Too often we are pressured by the happy Christian culture to mask true emotions regarding death and some of the other pains of life. This first-person account has a credibility that mere theorists miss. I especially appreciate that the book affirms the local church family as a safe place to hurt. Whenever the reading led me to tears, I felt good to be weeping with another who weeps (as the Scripture commands us). Thank you, Pastor Gary, for teaching us to be fully human Christians! **—Dr. Kevin Smith, Professor, School of Theology, Southern Baptist Theological Seminary**

I walked with Gary and Freda through the difficult days of their pilgrimage of love. I then watched closely as the even more difficult time of separation came. I agonized with Gary, prayed fervently (yes I worried about him), and then I watched him begin to rise up out of the emotional abyss. I told him he needed to tell his story in order to bless many others who have to walk this bereavement road. If you or someone you know is hurting, this is the book that can help. **—John Marshall**

Anyone who knew Pastor Gary Crawford and his wife Freda could see that they were on a "pilgrimage of love" every day. It showed in the way they looked at each other, the way they supported each other in ministry, and the way they raised their children. They traveled together through the years of Freda's illness with unbelievable grace and still stayed strong for their family and for the church ministries. During the two years since Freda's death, those of us who love Pastor Gary have watched him struggle to continue that pilgrimage alone . . . and yet not alone. He has relied on his strong faith and on his memories of his life with Freda. His struggles, his moments of doubt, his transparency, his victories, and his ability to stay strong in the midst of overwhelming grief will inspire all those seeking to find strength in the midst of loss or difficulty. — **Fran Terhune**

It was a real highlight for me to read *Grieving: My Pilgrimage of Love*. I was blessed, challenged, and encouraged by it. What a fresh reminder of God's individual and incredible love for us, as well as a challenge to my own life and marriage as I read how deeply committed Gary and Freda were, so closely knitted together and deeply in love. In our day, that is often not the case. This would be an incredible read for young marrieds, middle age and senior adult couples as a challenge to them and their relationships. It is definitely a book those dealing with grief *need* to read, and follow the example and admonitions that are so clearly laid out. —**Jim Law**

Grieving: My Pilgrimage of Love, the latest book from the fertile mind of Pastor Gary Crawford, is a story that brings the tributaries of life to flow as one river. That river is love. When that love is gone from our presence, the river still flows but often cuts a new course. The new course must include healing and hope, or the purpose for the river is lost. This is a fascinating read; Pastor Gary feels and writes with the same ink. —**John Sullivan, Executive Director-Treasurer, Florida Baptist Convention**

Dr. Gary Crawford brings a comprehensive understanding of the experience of grief with a message of hope to help face the adversities of life. *Grieving: My Pilgrimage of Love* is a solid, captivating, and genuine personal story that will help its readers sort through the trials of life and help find consolation and understanding, develop appreciation and endurance, and accomplish healing and closure through biblically-oriented guidance offered in this beautifully written masterpiece. I highly recommend

this book for readers seeking spiritual help to cope with grief.
— **Dr. Leonardo Rodriguez, Assistant Professor of Psychiatry, University of Florida College of Medicine.**

As a physician, I frequently counsel patients and families who have recently lost a loved one. Our culture makes it difficult to grieve openly, and we find, after we have lost someone very important to us, that relationships in life are what count most. We may have regrets and wish we could go back in time and do things differently, but this is impossible. In his book, *Grieving: My Pilgrimage of Love*, Gary Crawford shares his personal journey in search of answers after the love of his life, Freda, passed on after a prolonged illness. Gary is the pastor of a large church in Gainesville, Florida and the book is written from a Christian perspective. He is also the father of two children, and he shares how the love of his family defined the quality of his life. He also shares how tough times will reveal the strength of family and who one's real friends are. We all will suffer losses of loved ones. This is part of life. It is the hope of the author that the readers will find encouragement and strength as they deal with their own grief and loneliness, and through their own journeys learn positive lessons about life and love. It is an honor to know this kind and compassionate man.
— **Robert A. Erickson, M.D., Friend and Physician**

Acknowledgements

I am indebted to many who were a part of enabling me to write this book. No one more so than Diane McAlhany, who typed and retyped this manuscript and always with a positive attitude and smile. She has been a wonderful assistant for years and remains so. And I count her a precious friend.

Dr. Fran Terhune is a long-time co-worker and friend. She is a scholar and a catalyst. She worked with my late wife to edit my book *In Celebration of Love, Marriage, and Sex* and has been instrumental in editing this one as well.

My wife Freda, of course, is the primary impetus for this writing. Even though she is not here to help edit—she remains the source of inspiration.

Special friends have walked with me during this pilgrimage of love. They have brought to me invaluable support and insight. To these "forever friends" I will ever be grateful. My hope is that our relationships will encourage you as they have me.

Dedication

to

My Family and Friends

Who Have Journeyed with Me

And to Those Who Will

Table of Contents

Part Four—The Gift of Love
What Ultimately Matters

Preface

A Personal and Transparent Journey

There are many well-researched books on grief. I have read many of them. In my study as a biologist, I looked at the physiological impact of grief. In my graduate work, I looked at the theology of grief. In my doctoral work—an integration of theology, psychology, and counseling—I looked at the personal and relational issues of grief. I am grateful for such opportunities, and these studies have helped me and enabled me to help others along the way, for which I am also grateful.

The idea of stages of grief was first suggested by Dr. Erich Lindemann, Professor of Psychiatry at Harvard University. He described grief in the article, "Symptomatology and Management of Acute Grief," published in 1944. In this remarkable study he identified the five stages he saw in grief: shock, denial, anger, mourning, and recovery. Some would not use the word "recovery" because it can be said that one never recovers from the death of a loved one. The loss changes our lives forever.

Others, such as Dr. Granger Westbury, in *Good Grief* published in 1962, have noted ten stages of grief: shock, emotional upheaval, depression, physical symptoms, panic, guilt, resentment, paralysis, hope, reality. There is also a differentiation between "normal" grief (usually lasting for two-five years) and "abnormal" grief in which a person gets stuck and cannot move forward in a healthy way.

While it is true, in a sense, that "every person must grieve in his or her own way," the stages of grief are common to us all. We move through these stages in our own way, according to personality and perhaps particular circumstances.

More important than grieving "in our own way" is to grieve biblically. The Bible says "... *we do not want you ... to grieve like the rest of men, who have no hope*" (I Thessalonians 4:13). What I have learned thus far about such grief is this: we grieve with the "presence" and help of the Holy Spirit (He comforts us and guides us); we grieve within the Body of Christ, the local church where we are to help one another; we seek to grieve honestly—sharing our fears, doubts, weakness, and perhaps poor choices. We grieve with hope, that is, with a confident assurance that though we will never get over the loss, we will go through the loss with the expectation that *" . . . in all things God works for the good of those who love him, who have been called according to his purpose"* (Romans 8:28). We grieve with the prayer that our grief will be used to help others. We are comforted with the commitment to find a way for our grief to be used to advance the gospel and to comfort others (see 2 Corinthians 1:4). We do all of this intentionally; we run toward the darkness instead of from the darkness. As we do, we meet the sun coming up and rediscover hope and life.

It is good to keep in mind that in reality grief does not occur in neat, well-defined stages. A person may go in and out of the various stages as he or she moves toward healing.

Grief is very personal, and there is not a magic formula or magical point when it is over. It has been termed *work* because each person must work through his or her own grief. Anyone who has been through it knows it is indeed work. Grief has been compared to peeling an onion: "It comes in layers, and you cry a lot."

As I have moved through my grief, I have noted the phases. They can probably be discerned in this record of my pilgrimage. Having a framework in which to put our pilgrimage is helpful. While I encourage you to read some of the more formal studies on grief, my approach is very personal.

This book, then, is not about research; it's about my own experience of grief in the loss of my wife, Freda, after her ten-year battle with multiple myeloma. Having shared a personal faith in Jesus Christ, thirty-nine years of marriage, two children, educational pursuits, teaching in the public arena, a pastoral ministry, and a love that held through failure and success, her loss was devastating. In a sense, her loss left my life an empty shell where she once lived, loved, and played. I had to find a way to manage my grief in a positive, productive way that, in the end, could be a help to others as well as to myself. This book is the story of that effort.

My grief, when it came at her loss, knocked me off my feet emotionally—not spiritually—not physically—not relationally, but emotionally. In my effort not only to recover but to become stronger through the process, I found those who wrote from experience, or talked with me from their own experience, were most helpful. If that is true for me—it may be true for you.

Our culture makes it difficult to grieve openly. We are forced, we think, to carry the grief within ourselves. It hasn't always been that way. There were traditions and rituals that allowed for a shared grief. Full mourning used to last a year and one day. Men wore black arm bands or maybe a black band around their hat. Women wore black crepe, a color that symbolized the absence of light and life. Even petticoats had to have a black ribbon sewn on the hem. There were veils, bonnets, and special mourning lace handkerchiefs that had black borders.

The second mourning phase lasted nine months. The dress could be lighter and some jewelry worn. The veil could be lifted. Half-mourning was the last stage and lasted three to six months. Again, the dress could be of brighter colors and the veil lifted.

Mourning traditions changed, out of necessity mostly. So many soldiers died in the Civil War that almost the entire South was in mourning. The morale of the people was being affected by the sight of black everywhere. Gradually, in large measure because of war, women went into the work place. That, too, caused changes in grieving traditions. Additionally, the dress for grieving could be expensive. For poor families, this cost could be a strain on resources. At the end of *The Wonderful Wizard of Oz*, Dorothy explains to Glenda, the Good Witch, that she must return home because her aunt and uncle couldn't afford to go into mourning for her because it was too expensive.

There was, of course, the downside of such rituals. Nevertheless, they communicated clearly respect for the grieving process, and that grief is not finished overnight. They allowed others to be alert and supportive and said, in general, that the reality of death was not taboo and to be denied, as in our present culture.

These practices at least exposed the grief and prompted the opportunity to share. Now we have a grief conspiracy of silence. We don't display it; we don't ask about it. We offer our sympathy immediately at the viewing or funeral, and then it's back to business as usual.

As one person who lost her husband decried, "Right after I lost my husband, I was surrounded by a lot of family and friends . . . then I felt that most people acted as if it were life as usual. About three months after my husband died, a good friend of mine asked, 'Don't you want to be married?' I just couldn't believe it. I still felt married. It made me feel that I was expected to be over my loss and getting on with my life."

These pages are about transparency, about community, about grief as a process, and a journey. The transparency may, at times, make you uncomfortable. It makes me uncomfortable. It doesn't fit the macho mold. I know about that life. I was raised in a tough environment (the punch thrown, the knife pulled, the gun leveled), and my military experience exposed me to the same. I have been at sea, in the mountains, in the jungles, and, oddly enough, in dangerous experiences in ministry. I know that side of life. But there is the other side—love, peace, gentleness, and quiet strength. This is the life Christ calls us to no matter the circumstances we experience. This is the side I want to share—though it is uncomfortable at times. I share because this is where grief takes us. It has been two years since Freda "went home to be with the Lord," as we who follow Christ would say. During these two years, I have stayed steady in ministry leadership to my beloved church family, have been involved in various mission commitments on several continents, and have walked with my family who journeyed through their own grief and shared mine. This is to say that I write "from the trench," not from a podium. I write from where you live, where you face your own challenges, where you deal with your own loss, and where you struggle to regain balance and hope.

I hope my journey can help you in your own.

Introduction

Falling in Love

The fall morning was bright and sunny and the air brisk. I had just finished piano and vocal lessons at the small community college in North Florida and was leaving the humanities building, walking over to the science building. As I headed down the sidewalk, I looked up and walking in the cool shadows of the pines, I saw Freda walking toward me. She was heading to the building I was leaving. She and I had known one another most of our lives—at a distance . . . a far distance. But this year we were in a biology class together and in a theatre play as well, and I found myself falling in love. I knew she had graduated at the top of her class in high school and was at college on a scholarship. When she was elected president of the student body, I realized she was a leader. Even then I thought she was "over my head." And she was. Still, I had hope.

Now, watching her walk toward me, I suddenly wanted to run toward her, and simultaneously to run from her. On the one hand I was pulled to her as if she were a powerful magnet I could not resist. On the other hand, I was overpowered by her presence and wanted to change direction to avoid her. After all, what would I say when I met her? My heart was pounding and felt as if it had been relocated to my throat. Wouldn't I stutter and stumble? And wouldn't she, with those big, brown, perceptive eyes, see through me and know—know that I was stunned by her beauty, her intellect, her status, and her character? Wouldn't she know I had a secret fantasy—a secret longing that she would fall in love with me and become mine?

Of course, she would know—and maybe say "NO!" What an intimidating risk I felt. But she was coming; we were about to meet head on. What then? I walked steadily toward her because I could do nothing other. The force of her presence overcame all other feelings at work within me. I didn't know then what I know now—this was a moment of destiny.

As the distance narrowed between us, her face came into view. On her face was the smile that I would come to so love. It was a smile of acceptance, assurance, and anticipation. Another few steps, and her eyes met mine. I didn't care that those big, brown, beautiful eyes could and would see through me. In fact, in my heart I wanted them to do just that. She must know what I felt; I must acknowledge what I felt. And, in that moment when she came into view, we both knew what we felt for each other and that this was, in fact, our destiny.

Freda was the *"wife of my youth"* (see Malachi 2:14). We were married thirty-nine wonderful years that were filled with opportunity, challenge, and change.

Forty years later, seven months after losing her, while on a boat deep in the jungles of the Western Amazon basin in Brazil, I wrote these words:

WHEN SHE CAME INTO VIEW

When she came into view that first day,
I knew she was the one.
What I saw was a lady, a lady
with the beauty of a rose in bloom.
When she came into view that wedding day,
I knew she was the right choice.
What I saw was a bride, a bride
with the love of a lifetime in her eyes.
When she came into view that special day,
with child in her arms,
I knew she would be a strong one.
What I saw was a mother, a mother
with a lifetime of nurture in her heart.
When she came into view that later day,
now with a bit of gray,
what I saw was a dream, a dream

of a lifetime come true.
When she came into view that hard day,
now with her soul away,
what I saw was a legacy, a legacy,
one lasting forever.
Love has lived, dreams have come true,
now there is a future without you.
When now she comes into view each new day,
her love is here to stay,
what I see is a gift, a gift
of love and grace.
Love lives on, dreams still come true,
because I, and others, have been loved by you.
With her by my side, dreams have come true.
We have climbed the mountains,
and we have crossed the seas.
We have seen the sun rise and the sun set
in a thousand different places and a thousand different colors.
With her by my side, there was a thrill in my day,
a peace in my night, and a bright hope in my tomorrow.
Now though, she is gone, her love still lives on,
her love still lives on.
When she came into view, my view changed forever . . .

When she came into my life—my life changed. The best of my life and accomplishments was a result of her influence. Now she is gone, and I grieve.

Grief—is it friend or foe? Is it an expression of love or selfishness? Is grief healthy or dangerous? After all, grieving persons often look the same—in the same way the crystal clear waters of the Florida Keys look. From the surface, they seem similar; but underneath, one area may be hosting beautiful coral and the other may be infested with sharks. So it is with grief, which can be healing, hellish, or dangerous, depending on how it is experienced and managed.

In a scene in the movie, *Lonesome Dove,* a six-hour western saga by Larry McMurtry, the cowboys drive the cattle herd across a swollen river. All is well except for one young man who gets caught in a nest of water moccasins and is bitten multiple times. His fate is sealed. Death is soon to come. He is dragged to shore and friends gather around him in his final moment. The sage, Captain Call, a former Texas Ranger, says, with lament in his voice, "He's right boys, the best thing you can do with death is ride off from it." I understand the sentiment, but you don't "ride off" from the loss of a loved one. If you try, it will follow you. In fact, the grief of it will hunt you down and will bite you with a venom no less deadly than that of a water moccasin. This is why I say that grief can be healing or hellish—depending on how it is managed.

These pages are about the pilgrimage of grief: a pilgrimage of love, for to love is to grieve when the loved one is lost. The deeper we love, the deeper and more painful we grieve.

Grief by its nature is dismal, dark, and difficult. Yet like dark, fertile soil, it can birth new life and is intended to do so. It's a dark womb where life is conceived—again. And the hope of life can be breathed—again.

Grief can become our teacher, teaching lessons of life and love that are pearls of great value. Grief can, and will, yield its treasure—but only to the one who mines its depths and follows its guidance back into the light.

These pages are about grief as friend, as healer. They are about hope and light.

This is why I'm writing. Having traveled this pilgrimage now for two years, I am convinced that grief can be my friend and healer. But this "surgery of the soul" is no less painful than the surgery of the body—maybe more so. Yet it offers healing for my broken heart. It offers hope for my future. I write now while on a plane to South Africa. This trip, too, is a part of my pilgrimage. You will, in the end, see why.

PART ONE
THE REALITY OF GRIEF

CHAPTER ONE
What Grief Is Like

A Profile of Grief

Loss. In death the loss is so permanent. The door is shut, bolted, and locked. Yes, as Christians we believe in Heaven and the reunion with a loved one who is a fellow believer. But that reunion is a promise—and forever different from our lives on Earth. Grief is about the here and now. It's about life not becoming *somewhat* different but *altogether* different.

Freda was a rock of faith and common sense. In the midst of her suffering, she was intellectually engaged, spirited, keen, reliable, and alert. Ask all those who stood beside her during the difficult times, and they will answer in one accord—*true*. That final morning she smelled the fresh cool of fall, gained her battle posture, and readied herself to enter the medical fray. Then she smiled, and now I wonder if her smile was not at me, but at the One who was about to beckon her; for within moments He took her home . . . Now she is gone from here, and things are altogether different.

Now I turn in bed in the morning to see that she is okay, only to be reminded she is not beside me. I call the home phone, and it is answered by her voice but not by her; I reach for a plate and know that my favorite meal, prepared only by her special recipe, is never again an option. I discover a bill unpaid because she always paid them. I turn in my mind to ask her counsel, and there is no response, only a memory. Yes, there is loss here and now; and it is permanent, feeling like an amputated limb that is gone.

Yes, grief differs. It seems to be in direct proportion to the capacity to love and the depth of love experienced. This is why one can throw off some loss in a moment and yet struggle unto death with another. Grief is the price of love. It is as one has said, the "curse of intimacy." Yet anyone who has the capacity and the opportunity to experience deep love would always choose the pain rather than forfeit the love, for love in the end claims us and compels us.

And so grief, in the end, may be the "pearl of love." Everything within me may scream, "Come back!" but she can't, she shouldn't—it wouldn't be good for her or for us. It is good for her to be in His presence. But now the grief . . .

What Does Grief Feel Like?

The experience of grief is not fear, but it feels like fear: a constant fluttering of the stomach, maybe a faint nausea, a fog of the mind that makes it difficult to focus. At times the feeling is a break from common-sense thinking. The feeling is a chaos with many impulses at once: it's a dance where the music has stopped, a dream that didn't come true, a flower where the bloom has fallen, a hole in the soul, a ripping of the heart, a ship loosed from its mooring, a rainbow that has disappeared behind a dark cloud, a dark hole that beckons, "come deeper." There is a vague but abiding sense of something amiss, something wrong. There is a feeling of being stripped of what is most beautiful and valuable in one's life. As Stephanie Ericsson says, "Grief is a tidal wave that overtakes you, smashes down upon you with unimaginable force, sweeps you into its darkness where you tumble and crash against unidentifiable surfaces, only to be thrown out on an unknown beach, bruised and reshaped—grief will make a new person of you—if it doesn't kill you."

Yes, there are the photographs, beautiful as they are; but I don't want a picture, I want her. It was Freda, in her many persons to me, that I loved, not just her picture or her image. When one of the children called me on my cell from our home phone, it came up on the screen as "Sweetheart" as it had been set to do. I was stunned for a second—is she calling—how is she calling? Yes, there are reminders, such as photographs, phone settings, and voice mail still with her voice; but I miss her with an ache of body and soul.

Grief feels like constant movement—nothing stays put—

like a winding path in a valley with an unexpected landscape around each corner, like walking in circles and praying to avoid a spiral. The first days after losing Freda, I felt as if I were caught in a current, sometimes being moved lazily along and then sometimes moving as in a torrent with sharp rocks, maybe being cut to pieces or drowning by the force upon me. When my granddad lost my grandmother after nearly sixty years of marriage, he said on the morning of her death, "I don't want to live any longer," and he didn't. Though in good health, he was gone within a month. Now I had a glimmer of understanding what he meant.

A friend sent me a text message asking, "Where are you?" My reply, "In a place I have not traveled before, where there are new discoveries by the hour—some frightening, some joyous. It's a journey I must complete."

These feelings of grief are powerful and can work for good or ill. While they may vary in intensity and duration according to the capacity to love and the depth of love experienced, they are more or less universal for us all, and that is why we can comfort one another *". . . with the comfort we ourselves have received from God"* (2 Corinthians 1:4).

CHAPTER TWO
The Onset of Grief: How It Started

Her fight was long—ten years. This writing doesn't address the grief that comes with a chronic and terminal illness of a loved one. It only speaks of the grief of final loss. But the last few months were especially difficult with one hospital stay, then another, but always with the relentless hope that the stay would be short and Freda would soon be back on her feet.

After the last stay in the local hospital, she was very weak. She spent one night at home, and then the next morning boarded a plane to Arkansas with oxygen by her side, the help of Eyrone Bush as her delightful and diligent nurse, and with my assistance. She made the flight miraculously well with her and Eyrone doing what they do best, talking non-stop. Each day Freda managed the rigorous testing at the Arkansas Cancer Research Center in Little Rock, which had been her primary place of treatment since the beginning. Why, because there was a dedicated physician, Dr. Bart Barlogie, who was (and remains) committed to finding a cure for multiple myeloma. The Research Center in Little Rock was the place where most of the research for this disease had been done and the home of the largest database for treatment. We believe her treatment there gave us an additional ten years together. We will always be grateful.

At the end of that week, she insisted I return for our special commitment day at Westside, the church I have pastored for thirty years in Gainesville, Florida. We were making financial commitments for our new Family Life Center. She wanted the pastor of the people to be present with them. She felt that was one way she could contribute to our future ministry, in addition to making our own financial commitment. I reluctantly returned home, and God's presence came in a special way that day to our church family.

Wrapping things up at the church in Gainesville, I left Tuesday, driving back to Little Rock, thinking we would need a vehicle for an extended stay. I drove through the rain all that afternoon and would have driven through the night, except she made me promise to stop and get some rest.

Our wedding had been taped on an old eight-inch reel and was rather miraculously preserved. Mike Ricks, the Associate Minister of Media at Westside Baptist Church, was kind enough to transfer it to a CD. My intention had been for us to listen to the ceremony with our children the previous August on our thirty-ninth anniversary, which had not been possible because of life as it had become. So I had packed it for Freda and me to listen to in Little Rock at the first opportunity. That evening, while staying at the La Quinta Hotel in Dothan, Alabama, I wrote her a letter I planned to share with her when we listened to our wedding ceremony. Here is that letter:

> *Sweetheart,*
>
> *When we said "I do," closed the deal with a kiss, and rode off into our future, I had no idea of the "ride" we would have. One may call it foolish, or presumptuous, or idealistic, but no one could call it boring. The ride together in life has been an adventure.*
>
> *Like a roller coaster, sometimes up and sometimes down, but always in motion. There has been the slow clank to the top with its anticipation, the fast spiral with its thrill, always a "hang on" kind of experience. There is more coming!*
>
> *That deal, closed with a kiss, placed us on an educational journey with a destination of two doctorates (actually your first was a PHT–"put hubby through"'). Yet, no book learning has taught me what I have learned from you. You have been my true graduate school, and what you have conferred can't be granted by text.*
>
> *That same deal, closed with a kiss, bore the fruit of two children, both attractive, bright, honest, and*

loving, who have now blessed us with more of the same in our grandchildren.

That same deal, closed with a kiss, put us on a path in ministry that has crossed the states and circled the globe. So much of God's created beauty we have either seen, smelled, climbed, crawled, or driven. We have seen the mountain tops, the valleys, the hills, the rivers, the streams, the deserts, the beaches, the glacier ice, the deep underwater, and the high blue sky. We have weathered the freezing cold, managed the humid heat, and enjoyed the cool between. Most importantly, we looked into the eyes of every race and creed and saw the longing in their eyes for a transcendent love and offered that in the person of Jesus Christ.

That same deal, closed with a kiss, has provided the highest ecstasies of life and some of the deepest sorrows and most powerful losses. In both the highs and lows, we were there together, hand-in-hand, sometimes sharing mingled tears of joy and sometimes hot tears of sadness. At times, our direction seemed clear and certain. At times, the path seemed obscure and uncertain. Nonetheless, somehow we remained on the same path helping each other along the way.

I have loved you, but have failed you in ways that leave regret. Yet I find comfort in the words you have spoken on more than one occasion—"We do the best we can with who we are at a given time." I wish I had been more much earlier in our ride together. I wish I were more now as we yet travel together. But whatever there was, whatever there is, your love claimed it and your love has made the most of it.

I cannot imagine a traveling companion who would have, could have offered more for the ride.

19

*The strength, the grace, the beauty, the encourage-
ment, the hope ultimately to arrive at our destiny
could not have been equaled. You have defined
the standard. Your love has been a pearl, your
strength my haven, your never-ending hope my
rainbow. The light on my face has often been only
a reflection of your smile. Your beauty has grown
ever more beautiful as I have grown more capable
of seeing what was always there. Funny, isn't it,
how that works!*

*We still travel together. Life holds no more
uncertainty now than it ever did. But perhaps now,
a bit weather-worn and wiser, we understand more
clearly that in the uncertainty of life, we find our
greatest opportunity and our deepest values.*

*It has been quite a ride "partner." Hang on, the
best is just ahead around the bend. I'm so glad we
"closed the deal" and sealed it with a kiss.*

I love you,
GARY (11/10/09, Dothan, Alabama)

I was up with the sun the next morning. I pressed through
one slow mile, it seemed, after another. Sometimes I had
trouble trusting my GPS, as I did trusting the outcome of her
treatment in Little Rock. Sometimes I thought there was rain
on the windshield only to discover it was tears in my eyes. Ten-
and-a-half hours later, watching the sun set beautifully on the
horizon behind Little Rock, I arrived at the Research Center
where Freda was still trying to finish her day of testing. She
was very ill. Paula Johns, the second nurse "angel" who traveled
to Little Rock to assist Freda, was by her side. Although so ill
and weak, Freda had said to Paula, "Get my make-up. Gary
will arrive soon." She never ceased in her effort to look her best
and to be her best.

Perhaps she needed to be hospitalized through the emer-
gency room that night, but Freda said that would require more

effort than for her to get back to our Little Rock home with our good friend, Bobbie Lowry. When we got her back and in bed in the midst of her nausea and weakness, she had not lost her wit. She said to Bobbie, with a sly grin, that she had "stood her up for dinner." (We had planned dinner together.)

She gradually felt a bit better; and we prayed together, including a prayer for our church family. The night was restless for us all, but she had regained some strength. When morning came, Paula helped her dress. We got her in the car, and she inquired of a neighbor friend, who had stopped by, how her son was doing. She talked of the beautiful day and was ready to face a battery of tests including a heart biopsy.

We arrived at the Center at 7:30 am. Paula and I helped Freda out of the car. She stood for a moment, commented again on the beautiful morning, smiled with her bright smile—as beautiful as the morning—then we sat her in the wheelchair. I leaned over and kissed her on the cheek saying, "I will see you in a minute" and left to park the car.

She commented to Paula about it being a bit cool as they entered the Center and moved toward the registration desk. The lady at the desk must have seen something in Freda's face and said to Paula, "Get her back into the room now." When I walked in five minutes later, the same lady told me to go quickly back and see the physician. I was met by a nurse and stopped from entering the room where physicians and other medical professionals already surrounded her, doing everything possible to establish a heartbeat. The nurse was kind, but firm and told me, "It doesn't look good," and asked me to be seated. She asked me about "heroic efforts" and about "life support." Decisions had to be made quickly. It was fortunate Freda and I had already discussed these decisions. I knew her wishes from the time that our attorney friend, Jim Larche, had come to the hospital while in our hometown of Gainesville to assist us in our Designation of Health Care Surrogate.

That being said and done, I still could hardly say "No" to the life support. The moment was agonizing, excruciating. I knew what she wanted under the circumstances. I knew the doctor had just said, "She has been too long without oxygen." I knew all of this and more—but letting go—forever? I prayed and asked for God's wisdom. I called our son John for his *presence* in this moment of decision; I wanted to call our daughter Christa, but time was gone. I simply said, "They have done the best they can—so has she." There was silence on the phone. There was agony. It was decision time. We both knew the answer. And with the strength I gained from his voice, the decision was made.

"May I see her," I asked the nurse. She said they would need a few moments. Those few moments seemed like an eternity. Paula came to my side. We prayed, we cried, we talked. I will always be grateful for her presence. Later Paula would write, "I am still in awe, even after two years. What a wonderful, strong, gracious woman she was, even when she was feeling so bad. I am the one who was truly blessed by her during that short week. I am a better person for that."

I called my sweet daughter. We cried. She comforted. She was ready to come to me.

As I entered the dimly lit room and saw her lifeless body lying on the sterile bed, my heart imploded with an emotional tsunami. I had lost the *"wife of my youth."* The door of life here on Earth had been slammed shut and double-locked. My heart screamed the words that Cade, our grandson, spoke with tears and muffled voice at her viewing, "I want her back." Falling to my knees beside her bed, I wrapped my arms around this "other part of me" and cried in anguish and agony of soul. Forty years of memories flashed through my mind—and now I had only memories left. The fight for life, fought with courage and resolve, was over. Our journey was done. Our family—what now? I grieved their loss as my own. I stayed for a long time. I could hardly bring myself to leave. I had to tear myself away. I would walk to the door, then walk back to her side—walk to the door, then back, until finally I had the resolve to leave. Leaving, I thought, "My God, how do I live without her?" She had sung many times, the song, "Oh How I Want to Know You

More." One line of that song says, "I would give my final breath to know Your death and resurrection." She died and now she knows, for to be " . . . *absent from the body is to be present with the Lord"* (2 Corinthians 5:8, KJV).

That morning she had entered the Center like a lady strolling into a garden—beautiful and full of grace. But she also entered as a fighter into the ring for one more round. There she was, "tough and tender" with "grit and grace," my beloved Freda. God said in His sovereign purpose. "Enough. I call the fight. You have won. Come home." She *"fought the good fight,"* she *"finished the race,"* she *"kept the faith,"* and now she has received *"the crown of righteousness"* (2 Timothy 4:7-8).

Days before, various friends had raised the question when she had made the decision to return to Little Rock: "Why is she doing this, Gary?" That is, why is she continuing to fight? The answer was simple: Isn't that what a champion does? She fought because of her faith, her courage, her love of life, and her love for family and ministry. Freda not only modeled *how* to live, she showed us *how to die*. Among her comforts was Psalm 71:5-6:

"For you have been my hope, O Sovereign Lord, my confidence since my youth. From birth I have relied on you; you brought me forth from my mother's womb. I will ever praise you."

She did!

I went to the prayer chapel there in the Center, where I had spent so much time over the years either praying or working or both. The room was so familiar: the desk, the open Bible, the chairs, the lamp, the quietness. I sank to my knees. I thanked God for Freda, for all the medical personnel there and those in Gainesville who had cared for her. I thanked, in prayer, our church family, who had walked with us, and for friends who had encouraged us.

Our son John arrived by 3:30 that afternoon, and before nightfall we left for Gainesville to be with family. (The entire family had already made arrangements to arrive with him, but it was best that I go to them.) Later, John would write these words about the trip:

"The Trip Home"

Backing out of the driveway I caught a glimpse of her walker in the rearview mirror.

Within just hours I'd come to hate the word "was"; its reality couldn't be any clearer.

Miles and time stood between us and the rest of her loved ones as we drove out of Little Rock.

I was a stranger in a strange town, but Dad stared as we drove out of town, past the healing home away from home.

As Dad clenched his fist and beat the air, I punched the gas, anxious and scared.

Mom was gone, and we were on a long, long trip back home.

Blues were alive in Memphis that night as we found our way to a hotel room.

I needed my wife, Tina, and we both needed Mamma. Our beds were too big, and tomorrow couldn't come too soon.

I wondered how much Daddy would cry that night.

I wondered if I could be the right friend.

I wondered what the night would feel like with Mamma not in the world, and when the night would end.

Mamma was gone, and we were on a long, long trip back home.

I thought one last time about Memphis lights, stared at the blues and faced the night.

Morning dawned with Mom still gone. Time is funny when you feel all alone, but Dad was there and I was there, and the sun seemed out of place that day.

Clouds were thick on that bright and beautiful day, and we found that Tupelo was a good place to cry. We talked about arrangements in an awkward *way, and Dad took calls as time went by.*

It's funny how dying looks beautiful on the leaves of a tree,

And Alabama hills were dressed in cotton white as far as the eye could see.

Mom was beautiful and now, no doubt dressed in white. I know everything in heaven seems just right,

But Mamma was gone, and we were on a long, long trip back home.

Night fell hard again and my head felt heavy from dammed-up tears,

I turned up the music in place of cryin' as we passed the hours that seemed like years.

We sat still and quiet while Jackson Browne drowned out the hum of the road.

He sang about the load out, and something in those words rang true about the end of the show.

Mamma was gone and we neared the end of our long, long trip back home.

As we pulled in the same driveway where I had last told her goodbye,

My nervous regret would not allow me to cry.

I thought of Dad and his life all alone, about how he would miss her voice in his empty home.

Damn time for never letting you go the other way.

The present is the past tomorrow; everything seems distant, but then it's gone.

Mamma was gone. She had finished her short trip back home.

A few days later, after our return, I made this journal entry:

These last few days have looked much as usual from the outside, but from the inside, I feel as if I am separated from all around me by a thin sheet of glass. Voices seem muffled. The days seem endless, yet fleeting; and I grieve each day thinking of the grief of tomorrow.

Her absence is like a quilt that blankets everything. Life is not a little different, it is altogether different. Life, right now, feels like an empty stage with no script, like learning to walk again after paralysis. Like the boat at sea with two engines pressing toward shore, when suddenly one is lost, the other must strain its way to the harbor.

Once boundless energy is replaced now by loathe of effort. Clarity and focus are now a blur and replaced by uncertainty. My grief moves me from one place to another, causing me not to know where I stand or when I will stand on solid footing again. But I know that my grief, in God's grace, will do its work; and the memory that turns me in a second into a whimpering child will, in time, turn my weakness into strength. Days that now seem endless will again be filled with purpose. The empty stage will have a new script; my walking will become steady; energy will return; focus will become laser; and my footing will become secure. How do I know this even when I cannot feel this certainty or yet see how this can be true? Because God has said, "For I know the plans I have for you . . . plans to prosper you and not to harm you, plans to give you hope and a future" *(Jeremiah 29:11). But in my early days with my new companion of grief, this was not a statement of feeling, but of faith.*

No, I didn't have the opportunity to share the letter with her I had written on my way back to her in Little Rock, nor did we have the opportunity to share our wedding tape and celebrate as I had hoped. Yes, that was a deep disappointment, a regret. But the letter was read at her "Celebration of Life" service. The wedding tape the children and I shared that Thanksgiving as we spent a few days together in the mountains which Freda so loved. It was a time of sharing memories and celebrating a woman of strong faith and one who had an unconditional love for her family.

This Thanksgiving trip with the family was the beginning of a pilgrimage . . .

PART TWO
THE PILGRIMAGE OF GRIEF
The Most Significant Places Revisited

CHAPTER THREE
Where It All Started

Faith empowers us to engage our grief. It enables us to face it so it may do its good work of healing and restoration. I knew I needed to engage my own grief. I didn't want to—I needed to.

How do we engage our grief? For me, it was an intentional pilgrimage to the most significant places that marked the ages and stages of our lives. The places of my pilgrimage were not chronological as Freda and I lived them, but rather are described in the order of my visits. Come with me and see; you too may find strength for your own journey and hope for your future.

Where It All Began—College
December 2009

In the cool of December, a few weeks after her loss, I began this journey by going to the place where it all began with Freda and me—and to the place where it all ended, at least for this life.

I took the long way there by way of my grandparents' house. It seemed like only yesterday that I found warmth and security in their home of love. I was reminded of the brevity of life, as the Bible says, it is but *"a vapour"* (see James 4:14, KJV). Then past the old house where Mrs. Lamb taught me my first piano lesson, then to the old home place, my birthplace now called Crawford Pointe, then by the house of my first remembered childhood friend, all the while listening to the gifted and accomplished Andrea Bocelli, the blind Italian concert artist singing the melodies of faith and Christmas.

Arriving at the back entrance to the college Freda and I both attended, I pulled over beside the road. I felt my heart begin to hasten its pace in anticipation. There was excitement as I remembered the embryonic feelings of first love. There was longing as I missed her presence and a bit of dread and fear as I knew the dam of emotion was about to break.

That long ago morning, when rounding the curve to the

entrance of the school in my prized Pontiac GTO, I was playing the song that became our song, "This Guy's in Love with
You." So I placed the CD in the player and pulled back on the
road. As I rounded the curve with "This Guy's in Love with
You" playing in my ear, all the memories of first love surfaced
with the clear understanding that life together was over, and
the dam broke. I let it flood—it needed to happen.

Freda and I had visited the school together two years
before her death. That day had been sunny and bright. I wrote
about it in my book, *In Celebration of Love, Marriage, and Sex:
A Journey Through the Song of Solomon*. Today it was overcast
and cold. I took the same route around campus as with Freda,
revisiting each place. First, the music building where I sang
"The Impossible Dream," much of which became true with the
empowerment of Freda. Standing there, the question came to
me, "What is the impossible dream now?" How was I going
to live without the impossible dream of having Freda with me
here on Earth? How was it going to be possible to live with my
all-consuming grief?

Next, to the classroom where I gave my first speech, I stood
in the exact same place and began to feel my heart beat faster
and my palms sweat as they did the first time. Now forty years
later, I have stood in places and settings around the world, but
standing there again, the question came to me, "Where do
I stand now?" As I left the classroom and walked across campus,
the thought came to me that Freda had proven to be my best
education. As students passed by, I wondered what their future
held, and if they would have someone like Freda in their lives.

Arriving at the science building where Freda and I had
studied together, I saw a memorial on the wall to Dr. Don
Klinepeter. I remember him as the one who said to me after
the sudden loss of my mother, who was then thirty-four (and
I was eighteen), to "Go to the creek bank and think for a while."
I did and there made some decisions that would redirect my life.

The library, filled with books, only held one fascination—
the table where Freda and I had once sat and studied. Okay,

talked! Then, just outside the gym, I stood where she and I had exchanged the question on our last visit there, "How did your time here change you?" My reply in part was, "Here you came into my life, and that changed everything." Looking on the wall in the administration building and seeing the distinguished alumni photos on the wall, I wondered why she was not there. Then back in the arts building standing in the restroom, I looked in the mirror, where on the earlier visit the question had come to me, seemingly with force but out of nowhere, "What have you done with your life?" Now though, the question became, "What will you do with your life?"

Wanting to evade a definitive moment, I walked back to the center of the campus and sat on an iron bench. The question kept pressing on my mind, but without response. Then I noticed two squirrels scouring for nuts, and with this simple observation of two small creatures preparing for the winter, intent on survival, I knew. The answer to my demanding question came. What will I do with my life now? I will take care of my immediate needs; then answers will come in the spring.

I had completed what I had come to do: to face my past and my future. Yet, I found it difficult to leave. It seemed that in leaving, I was leaving her, *much as it seemed on the morning of her passing* when I found it so difficult to force myself to leave the room where her body lay—although I knew she had already left, for as the Bible says, " . . . *to be absent from the body is to be present with the Lord*" (2 Corinthians 5:8).

I left listening to "This Guy's in Love with You," thinking, this guy is still in love with you.

I drove to the nearby cemetery and turned to walk toward the most difficult task before me—to visit her gravesite. The cemetery is behind the church where we both grew up: we came to Christ here, were baptized here, and members of family are buried here. As I walked to the resting place of my beloved, the wind was blowing in my face and the air had become damp. The flowers, given by gracious family and friends, were beginning to fade, and some had fallen over. I picked them up, arranged them as best as possible, and knelt beside the stone which had these words, among others, engraved upon it:

"How delightful is your love, my friend, my bride" (Song of Solomon 4:10).

Freda and I met and talked. In person? Of course not. With audible voice? Only mine. But after years of sharing thoughts and feelings, exploring convictions and values, of sometimes passionate and sometimes relaxed dialogue, we could now talk. You understand, don't you?

I asked out loud though in a strained mumble, "What will I do with my life now that I am without you?" Here is what I heard her say: "Remember life is an adventure. Love our family, give your best, and rely on the One who made us and joined us, and go live—live the next impossible dream." These words from her were clear, but in my heart I knew I didn't even know how to begin.

"How do I let you go?" I cried. "I am home," she said. "I am better. You can one day join me and others whom you love who are here with me, but now see what I have left you—live for it—make the most of it, and remember I love you." Well, "Okay," I thought to myself, "I see what I need to do; now I must depend on Him to enable me to do it—whether I want to or not."

I took a deep breath, told her that all my best moments, best accomplishments, and best memories I lay at her feet. I thanked her for her life of love, and told her, "This guy is still in love with you." Then I walked toward learning to dream again, live again, accomplish again. Was the grief finished? Oh no, it had only been started in the hope of finding healing and health.

My personal grief is but a speck in the universe. It's only the point of a needle. But perhaps in my grief, you can find some strength for your own—some recognition of the truth that the God of all comfort, *"comforts us in all our troubles, so that we can comfort those in any trouble with the comfort we ourselves have received from God"* (2 Corinthians 1:4).

Glimpses of Healing

There are momentary glimpses of a reprieve from grief. They come quietly as the dawn and with surprise. They come in a good night's sleep after many restless nights. Maybe after confronting the terror of the dark night of the soul, the moment of reprieve opens the door that passionate grief closed. Maybe help cannot be received when there is nothing but a cry for help in the midst of the cutting knife of sorrow. As has been said, "Perhaps your own repeated cries deafen you to the voice you hoped to hear." Like the drowning person who cannot be saved because of his flailing, we cannot be helped because of our emotional and spiritual flailings. Maybe the glimpses are simply a gift from God, a taste of healing to come, an encouragement. Whenever they come, wherever and why, they unlock that bolted door, and there seems to be the prospect of companionship with the loved one again—not an image, not a photograph, but a personal presence. A smile is almost birthed again.

These glimpses at once bring me to a deeper sense of intimacy with Him again. Not only do I experience *her* again, but Him, the giver of life and love. Words of praise begin to move softly across my lips. They go first to Him as the giver, then to *her* as the gift. She is in His hand and so am I. If both are there, then love, intimacy, hope, and the future are certain . . . as certain as the Resurrection. I need Him, not an image of Him, not a photograph of Him, but Him. And I have Him, not a doctrine, not a theological idea, but Him. I do have Him—that is the reality of the Incarnation; that is the reality of the Holy Spirit, and that is the power of God. He is the healer; He is the answer; and He is the future. If I have Him, I have Freda and all loved ones who are in Him.

I am not a newbie to grief. My beautiful young mother, my precious grandparents, aunts and uncles, and some loyal friends, they have all gone before me, and I have pined for their passing. But if I have Him, I have them. Does *that* make the pain of grief an ill effect? No. We grieve, but not as those who have no hope (see I Thessalonians 4:13). Does that make the work of healing unnecessary? No, it gives the work purpose and direction. Does that dry every tear and remove every cloud? No—but it puts a rainbow in sight. Grief, in the end, like all of life, is not about us. No, it's not. It's about God in us through faith in Jesus Christ. It's about being chiseled, one hard blow after another, into the character and love of Christ. It's about being a channel of comfort. It's about a transcendent purpose. It's about life, not death. And because it is, grief can become our teacher.

Insights I am Learning From Grief

- Loss is real; it's painful, and it's permanent. Life will for-ever be different. It's not a video game where you lose life or take life without pain. It's not a movie where you can change the scene by a touch of the control if you don't like it. It's real; it's painful; and it's permanent with eternal consequences. *"For the wages of sin is death, but the gift of God is eternal life in Jesus Christ our Lord,"* the Bible says (Romans 6:23).

- Our grief must be faced. It seems a terrible and frightening foe. But to withdraw from it is eventually to be overcome by it and fall to its sword. The Bible says, *"For God did not give us a spirit of timidity, but a spirit of power, of love and of self-discipline"* (2 Timothy 1:7). In God's strength the grief must fall on the sword of faith and courage.

- Grief is intended to be a friend. It is God's healing process. It is meant to be the pearl of love, not the curse of intimacy. We " . . . *approach the throne of grace with confidence, so that we may receive mercy and find grace to help us in our time of need"* (Hebrews 4:16). Healing is a gift. We can nurture and nurse; but in the end, as with the body, healing of the soul is a gift from the Giver of life.

- Grief is a stewardship. It must not be wasted. Freda saw her illness this way—a ministry, she called it. *That* is what she made it: a blessing to thousands around the world, as testified by those from many states and most continents.

And we must see our grief as such a stewardship, that it may become a comfort and strength to others.

- We need one another. That is the way God designed us and especially so in the Body of Christ where we have become one in Christ. We are to be a healing community. We are not to be a people to criticize, slander, backbite, and create dissension. These things God hates, the Bible says (see Proverbs 6:17-19). God will judge such ungodly behavior. We are to be a healing community of love, grace, truth, and encouragement.

- Grief is an anvil, a crucible. Under the pressure of the hammer, it reveals truths about ourselves. These can be denied, or acknowledged and learned from. Positive change can occur. We can become more than we were before. That's called spiritual growth and that is God's intention. Otherwise, our faith is really a house of cards.

But you have your own grief: the loss of a loved one, the death of a marriage, the brokenness of a family, the loss of a job, the besetting of a disease, the disloyalty of a friend, or something else. Your heart is broken and maybe your dreams. I want you to have, if nothing more, a glimpse of hope, of healing. I want you to see the Healer, the hope of Christ Himself. When you do, a smile will be birthed and celebration is just around the corner. But this healing is not without its setbacks, and it has a stop and go nature to it, as you will see in the next experience.

CHAPTER FOUR
A Cold Winter

Arnold, Missouri
February 25, 2010

Today was a hard day. Maybe a spillover from last Sunday—Valentine's Day. I was at First Baptist Church of Arnold, Missouri to speak at a Global Missions Conference. Arnold is about two hours away from Ft. Leonard Wood, where I was at boot camp in 1968. It was while there that Freda and I wrote most of our love letters to one another. It was there I decided that if I survived the winter I would ask her to marry me. I did survive, and I did ask her hand in marriage, which was the second best decision of my life—the first being to accept Jesus Christ as my Savior.

I wish I had taken another day to remain in Missouri and visit Ft. Leonard Wood and to relive some of the memories, but I felt the press to return for ministry with my church family.

Some days are more difficult than others, but the ache of soul is a constant presence and on some days becomes a bleeding of the soul. That was true today—three months and two days from the day I lost the love of my life. Her presence was everywhere, yet she was not present, and the absolute sense of profound *aloneness* gripped me like a vise.

In some ways this business of living without the other half of my being seems to be getting harder, not easier. Why is this?

I awakened this morning and said "Good morning" to her as if she were there beside me, but she wasn't. I dropped off some kitchen stools at home, stools I know she had wanted and said, "Sweetheart, that's the best I could do. I hope you like them."

Then this evening, I left the office about 6:00 pm. I started the engine of my Tahoe, but when I thought of going to a home without her, I leaned over the steering wheel and wept uncontrollably. When I finally arrived home and walked in the door, the one who made it home was not there.

So why does it seem harder when it is supposed to be getting easier? Only one reason: the reality of life without the one who loved so deeply, with such loyalty and steadfastness, under any and all circumstances with an immovable love. Her love survived and even thrived in the most difficult challenges of life, while embracing the greatest opportunities, such as children, accomplishment, and adventure. Yes, the progressive realization that such a love is gone—that's the answer to the question. The influence of such love goes on, but the person is gone for good. Life looks different, feels different—is different.

Today was black and white—not color. Today I moved through my responsibilities and challenges by sheer resolve. I know I must not allow the disappointments and hurts of life to diminish my own strength and thus allow my decisions to be controlled by my feelings.

Today I celebrated what I had; yet at the same time I longed for that which I can never have again.

It's not that I live with that feeling every day. I believe in tomorrow. I remind myself of that again and again, and I know it to be true. The sun will break through the clouds; color in life will return; the pieces of my soul will reorder themselves; my being without its other half will stabilize. This is God's promise and the work of His grace. I believe it to be true.

My challenge, in the midst of this, is to hold steady, live well, dream again, and dare to do what I haven't yet done and become who I am yet to be. Anchored in God's grace, by a multigenerational family of love that stands with me, by a calling that transcends all of the vicissitudes of life, and by a community of faith, like my church family, I will continue to journey through my grief to become who it is teaching me to be. I believe that means becoming a person of greater understanding, strength, and compassion, having a larger capacity to love, and deeper insights for living.

I may feel alone now, but I am not. I am certainly not alone in the challenges of life. People all around me are cut asunder by the realities of life in a fallen world. If my grief, well done, can somehow encourage and serve them, then it is worth it.

Now it is the end of this hard day. I can sit in front of the fireplace she and I enjoyed together and see within the flame the flicker of her smile and hope for a better day tomorrow.

There will be more days like this one. But I have learned that if you expect days that are hard, that are black and white with little or no color, they become easier and more instructive.

This being said, one of my most challenging and rewarding encounters with grief was just ahead.

CHAPTER FIVE
The Letters

St. Augustine
April 12, 2010

It has been five months since Freda went to a far better place. These months have been intense with family and ministry. Now a few days of vacation—a breather. In keeping with my commitment to grieve intentionally, I made a trip to St. Augustine, the place of our honeymoon.

I brought the letters, maybe 150 or more. Somehow we kept them over multiple moves and forty-plus years. The first year we dated, I was called to spend time in the military. Then when I returned, she had moved to another location to pursue her education at the university there. So for two years there was a constant writing of letters, and then on and off for the next few years. I thought I had lost the letters; but just before leaving on this trip, I discovered them. Now I intended to read them.

They are a time machine into the past: forty years before me in one day. As I read, one after another, sometimes I can't seem to breathe for the pain of seeing what I have lost. Reading her words is sometimes heaven, and sometimes hell. The love of my life is gone. She is not coming back. I must learn how to live without her. But I don't want to! God help me, for I must, if I am to live again.

I have captured today from those letters, these precious realities about our love:
- Our love was real—with her I discovered the meaning of love.
- Our love was intense from the beginning.
- Our love was of God.
- Our love held in spite of the storms.
- Our love beckoned—no demanded—our best.
- Our love grew through failure as well as success.

- Our love can never be replaced.
- Our love lives on.
- Our love was not perfect, but we were both embraced by the perfect love of Christ.

This is what I have been reminded of today about our life together:
- We must build the world we want to live in.
- Faith in Christ is the only hope for the best in life.
- We should live with passion.
- Mistakes are made by all and can be valuable for growth and change.
- Forgiveness is non-negotiable in love.

Five of the most important things she said to me:
- "I love you."
- "I am proud of you."
- "We do the best we can with who we are at a given time."
- "We must build the world we want."
- "Don't be afraid of the future."

What a day of memory, reflection, evaluation, regret, gratitude, and hope! I felt drained and dry like a swamp during drought. I felt limp like a washcloth that had been squeezed.

In need of fresh air, I walked to the beach. It was late afternoon. The waves were strong. I stood on the edge where water met sand. I was overcome with all the realities of life, the questions, the pain. I began to pray. I prayed for forgiveness, for healing, for strength, for wisdom, counting on the Lord's gracious response. I drew a line in the sand and placed there my failures of forgiveness, her suffering and struggle for final healing, every difficult, disappointing, confusing experience of the past, Westside Baptist Church and her ministry, and the future—all for God's gracious favor.

As soon as I had placed them there, a wave came quite unexpectedly and washed the line away. In that moment I found the symbol of God's grace, forgiveness, restoration, and future hope: a defining moment of peace.

Refreshed, I left for the motel where Freda and I had spent the second night of our honeymoon. At dusk I sat in front of Room 126, the room where we stayed that night. Young love, so exciting, so perplexing, so tantalizing. I sat in my Tahoe and listened to the CD she recorded—her beautiful singing voice, her lovely pure tone on *God's Sustaining Grace*. Phrases from the songs gripped me: "All my earthly wanderings melt into your love," "looking back His love and mercy I see," "He has been faithful to me," "touch through me," "open door."

Each of the songs brought a host of memories and images, filled with her faith, grace, and gracefulness. Darkness then fell, but I could hardly make myself leave. I wanted to start life with her all over again. I wanted to do some things better and some things differently. I wanted to be stronger from the beginning. I wanted to give what I couldn't then. But that couldn't happen. Yet I realized I can treasure what we did have.

The years have come and gone. Her time was cut short, it seems to me. But I know that is a limited perspective. That's the conclusion from a finite vantage point. Here's the deal: forty years ago God brought a young man and a young woman together—"a country boy and a country girl"—united them in life and purpose and promised from here, anywhere, and that's what we did. Our ministry to bring the hope of Christ to all people literally took us around the world. It was quite a ride together. In my opinion it was over too soon.

Now I wonder; I ponder; I search. I don't know all the answers, but I know this: Each day offers its own opportunity. We best make the most of it. And I know this—she said it—she wrote it: "We must build our world, the one we want to live in and leave." The statement implies work and faith. It calls for courage, planning, and commitment. Therefore, while I wonder, ponder, and search, I carry with me the memory of that day standing before our honeymoon cottage. I know I must build on this legacy made sacred by love. We began as two lovers, then one marriage, now a multi-generational family: this *is* her love and legacy and my opportunity and commitment for the future.

As we deal with our grief, one thing becomes clear. We must somehow deal, in a healthy way, with our past. There is no perfect life, therefore, no perfect past. It is likely there will always be some measure of regret. Maybe that is the reason one stage of grief has been identified as "guilt." It is essential to come to grips with this so there can come a time of peace within one's heart and mind. As one belonging to Christ, we can experience His forgiveness: *"If we confess our sins, he is faithful and just and will forgive us our sins and purify us from all unrighteousness"* (1 John 1:9). We can claim the promise that *" . . . in all things God works for the good of those who love him, who have been called according to his purpose"* (Romans 8:28). This is His gift of love to us, and one we can extend to others.

This love enables us to begin to do the hard work of "building the world we want to live in" after we have had our previous way of life crumble before us. While it requires hard work with faith and courage, a new life will begin to take shape.

But as you will see, I would come to ask myself at the next step in my pilgrimage, "Am I chasing Freda?"

CHAPTER SIX
A Mountain Lake

Lake Lure
September 25, 2010

It must have been 1985 when Freda, our children Christa and John, and I first visited Lake Lure. It was at the invitation of my sister and her husband, Jim and Rita Paladino—a free weekend to consider a timeshare. The place was beautiful. A large lake surrounded by foothills and mountains, green that summer, sometimes with sunshine reflecting off the leaves and sometimes covered by clouds that had fallen below the tree line. The winding roads, meadow pastures, and cattle and horses on the hillside made it almost like a fantasy paradise. Little did we realize that much of our future travel would be influenced by that weekend.

We had a great time swimming, exploring, and climbing the steep hills covered with leaves, rock, and fallen trees. We had agreed to take a sales tour, and we did. The question of whether to buy was a difficult one. We postponed the decision, asking for the night to think it through. The main attraction was the provision that we could trade weeks at places across the U.S. and around the world. I remember Freda and I lay in bed talking, after the fun and frolic with the children, about the pros and cons of this purchase. We wanted it for our family, but didn't know how we would pay for it. We prayed and agreed that we would each share our perspective the next morning. Before breakfast, we talked, and both felt we should make *the* buy.

Later that morning, we signed the papers. I said to the young man who was the sales representative, "I have listened to you, now would you listen to me about faith?" He agreed. I told him about the love of Christ. He prayed to receive Christ sitting there in the office. It was a sweet moment and seemed to give the whole deal a transcendent purpose.

The decision that day shaped much of our travel for the

future. I had a goal to have the family in fifty states and six countries by the time the children graduated from high school. We came close, having visited forty-seven states and six countries. These experiences were exciting, and the memories invaluable. Freda so enjoyed traveling and found joy in the places of indescribable beauty that we saw, some enchanted, it seemed. We both appreciated the educational opportunities for all of us, as well as the sheer adventure of it all. She was a navigator par excellence. With map and travel guide in hand, we traveled America and Europe, seeing some of the great cities of the world as well as traveling back roads of mountains, valleys, rainforests, deserts, and scenic routes by the sea. I will always be grateful for the decision in Lake Lure in 1985.

Now, I arrive here at Lake Lure again, but this time without her. It seems there is rain on the windshield, but no—only tears in my eyes. (I know I have said that before.) Tears of gratitude, joy, and, of course, sadness. Everything is here, and more, except one thing—the love and strength of my life. Yet her presence is everywhere like the misty haze that lies across the lake.

A strange thought came to mind, "Have I been chasing Freda these last months?" Since her loss, I have traveled to Lake City Community College where we fell in love; to Florida State University where she studied the year before our marriage; to St Augustine, the place of our honeymoon; and to Milton, Florida, where we lived the first six years of our marriage when I studied at University of West Florida and where we gave birth to our children. Before the year ends, I plan to visit Texas, where we spent five formative years of study and ministry, and finally to Little Rock where our journey together ended.

This has been my plan to engage my grief in a productive way, celebrate wonderful memories, and somehow communicate to my loved ones a legacy to be remembered and a hope for the future.

Now in the midst of my travels, the question gripped my mind: "Am I chasing Freda?" Do I keep trying to find her where we had once been? Do I hope she will be at the next stop waving me down with that bright smile as big as ever, with her long hair that I loved to run my fingers through, blowing in the wind? Well, certainly there is a sense in which she meets me at each sacred place, but in memory only. I am grateful for all of those memories of love, adventure, and life. I find my hope in the conviction that, in time, I will go to meet her in a place far better to enjoy for eternity. Until then, she has left so much to live for—namely a faith, a work that matters in the ultimate sense, children, and grandchildren. In their faces, their eyes, their smiles, I see her life and love.

At bedtime, I was exhausted. The sleep was the best I'd had in months. I awakened to rain on the roof, a cherished sound from childhood. Remembering that there was no early morning commitment, I smiled to myself, pulled the covers tight, and nestled in the warmth.

Alice was with me (Freda's mother; I have always called her "Mom"), and we worshiped together that Sunday at Fairfield Mountain Chapel. Freda and I worshiped there on more than one occasion. The last time was in early spring of last year. Everette Chapman is pastor there, and that morning the theme of the service was joy. The service seemed designed especially for me. The music was moving and the message warm, funny at times, thought provoking, and inspiring. We met Pastor Chapman after the service. I saw the puzzled look on his face as I introduced Alice, explaining the loss of Freda. "I am sorry, so sorry," he said. "She was such an attractive lady and beautiful person." I replied, "Yes, in every way," I thought to myself. Yes, my golden package.

Mom and I left church for the Lake Lure Hotel. It was built in 1927 and boasted visits by presidential guests. It remains a place of historic beauty situated cozily at the base of the mountain and by the lakeshore. The lobby is filled with American and European antique musical instruments, paintings, and photography of the notable and notables. The food was delicious and the conversation with Mom enlightening.

Mom shared with me some pages from Freda's past. Freda

had written a paper for a competition in school about the oak tree she loved to visit behind their home for solitude and enjoyment. She said in her paper that she was "grateful for the freedom and opportunity for such simple pleasures in life." Mom also shared that Freda was voted "Most Likely to Succeed" her senior year. (She survived thirty-nine years with me—that's success!) Mom also lamented not having the funds, as a single mother, to buy Freda a yearbook that noted her achievements. Freda was asked to sing on Senior Day as well. She sang "Born Free" to a standing ovation!

Mom also reflected on the close relationship between Freda and her grandfather, whom Freda called "Big Daddy." Without a father to walk her down the aisle for marriage, she asked him to do so. Mom said, "Big Daddy thought Freda hung the moon, as she did him. He might not have walked anyone else down the aisle, but he would never have turned her down," Mom explained. I remember well that tall, lanky, kind man and will always be grateful for his deep love for Freda. As I think of our wedding day, I wish I could, as the song "Pilgrim" says, "Go back and hold her hand"—again.

It has been good and insightful to spend time with Mom. Only when we know something of a person's life and heart can we appreciate him or her. Otherwise, we form impressions and give responses that are based on perceived reality. That is always dangerous in relationships and a loss to all. I was also reminded that knowing our history is important. Without it, it's akin to not having a memory of yesterday. Without it, we have difficulty knowing who we are and where we are going.

It was my hope this trip would be good for Mom and for me. I knew it would please Freda, who loved her mother deeply. It was strange to be there with my mother-in-law. Life, it seems, shouldn't work that way but it does. Maybe by loving Mom, it was an act of loving Freda as well. Isn't that a principle of life—that we love *all* when we love *one*?

After lunch we rode through Chimney Rock. I had so many memories of the children here. I can't rid my stomach of the butterflies, nor erase the smile from my face—memories of the banana split at the ice cream shop, or skipping the rocks across the mountain stream.

Returning to the lake house, I sat by the windows overlooking the gully, listening to Keith Jarrett play the piano. I wrote with deep gratitude for the past blessings and with high hopes for the future. With that thought I could see Freda smile. As the song, "Pilgrim" says, "In their faces [the children] I see her again, in their eyes I see her again, in their smile I see her again." I sorely missed our children that day and couldn't wait to see them. I am so proud of them. So was Freda.

I also missed my church family. I can't believe for thirty years I've had the privilege to serve them as pastor. Still so much love to be shared, so much work to be done. That work will occupy much of my time. Family, church family, and friends—this is my life—life at its best.

I discovered that, as I spent time with Alice, I better understood the early life of Freda and of her family. Let me share a journal entry with you that will help you understand what I mean.

All are Welcome at Mamma's

Alice went with me to Lake Lure because, as she said, "I didn't want you to go alone." I'm glad she did. The time together helped me get to know a woman whom I have known most of my life. We know people to the degree that they want to be known, the degree we want to know them and invest the time and effort to do so. I'm glad I made the decision to invite her, and I'm glad she accepted. Snapshots can't replace experience, but here are a few snapshots of her that will give anyone with interest a glimpse of the mother of my bride.

On that Tuesday evening, we sat in the Point of View Restaurant overlooking Lake Lure. We sat at the same table, I believe, that Freda and I sat at in the spring of the year before. The sun was setting, and a soft glow had fallen across the water. We ordered pan-fried mountain trout. Wanting to know more about Alice and Freda, I began asking questions to which she readily responded.

Alice met Tony, Freda's father, in Jacksonville while attending a business school. She stayed in a boarding house and Tony lived next door. They met, fell in love, and were married in Jacksonville, for lack of funds to travel home. Tony's grandfather was of German descent, but his grandmother was Cherokee Indian. Tony's father left the family early on. As a result, Tony didn't know his dad. Later, his mom married a good and kind man of Italian descent, who adopted Tony and raised him with his other children.

Tony and Alice's dream was for a lifetime, but the dream lay broken in less than five years. "I was naïve," she said. "I thought marriage was for life. I thought you worked things out. That is the only model I ever knew." Tony left when Freda's brother Ronnie was two years old and just before the birth of Freda. He visited about a year later when Freda was just turning one. Thus, she never knew her father. Years later, when she discovered his location, she attempted to see him. She and I, along with Christa and John, stopped by his home outside of Atlanta. He had just died. "He got his act together, in time, and had a family of his own," Alice said with a hint of relief in her voice. Ironic, isn't it, that he was abandoned, only to abandon his own? Fortunate that the hole in Freda's heart (and Ronnie's) would be filled by a grandfather she knew—they all knew—as "Big Daddy," a man with a heart as big as his 6'5" lanky body. Freda often spoke of him with such endearment that everyone at once felt a deep gratitude to him.

"So, Mom, your greatest dream that was broken?" She replied, "My dream for marriage and family. The pain of its failure is unending." "And the greatest dream come true?" I asked. "My children," she said, without hesitation. Children she raised alone, except for family surrounding her, which provided support of immeasurable value.

The sun had set by now. Mountain shadows were falling across the lake like shadows that fall across our lives. The shadow of disappointment and pain, as well as shadows of love and hope. The mountain trout was delicious, but the food of the soul shared at the table was better still.

The day was bright. As the Tahoe hummed its way down our chosen path, Alice spoke of rebuilding her life. After the collapse of her marriage, she stood on her feet again. She stood by the strength of her values and with the help of family. She finished business school, and later while working, raising her children, and remaining active in ministry, she finished an AA Degree. That degree, in time, opened the door for a job with the Florida Department of Transportation. She made land acquisitions, closing multi-million dollar deals in a myriad of varied experiences with people—and all this while she supervised other agents in her division. She spoke vividly of the memories of many experiences and with a voice of accomplishment and satisfaction. I felt a sense of pride in this single mom who had trusted the Lord for opportunity and strength. To the chagrin of her supervisor, she retired. She retired with many congratulations and later an invitation to come back, which she did, part-time, and for only a while. She then retired for good, having worked to protect inherited property; she had built and paid for her own home and had the means to live independently, even while helping others along their way as well.

Chimney Rock has an elevation of 4,225 feet above sea level. We went there to see the mountain range from this high point of rock sticking out of the mountainside like a chimney sticking out from a house. The day was sparkling clear and the view breathtaking. I cherished the memory of this view with Freda, now *over twenty* years before. Opera House Rock was still higher. "Let's go higher," said this soon to be eighty-four-year-old young lady. "Are you sure?" I inquired. "Nothing tried, nothing gained," she replied with a smile and that settled it. And we did!

Then she saw it—one ledge higher yet. The gleam was in her eye. "No, let's don't do that today," I said, with a firm tone. That spirit, which has taken her a long way in life, still empowers her to teach, lead, care for others, support missionary work in the field, and will see her through to the end and into His hands.

We discovered, by accident, the home of Robert E. Lee, which was just a short distance from Hendersonville. It sits on a hill surrounded by tall pine, spruce, and oak trees and overlooks a pond with ripples, which were dancing across the surface. As I stood there gazing at the history of a nation, I felt gratitude for brave men and God's providence over our country. Members of our own family fought for the cause and led in battle during the Civil War, and other wars as well. That remembrance brought history home and into the present. I wished Freda could have shared the moment, and, of course, our children too. With Alice and me, we account for four generations since that "War for the soul of our nation."

The home of Carl Sandberg, known as "The Poet of the People" was a short distance from the home of Robert E. Lee. Sandberg's home is a large white house situated on a hill behind a pasture and overlooking its own lake. The home remains as it was when the great writer and his family lived there. The details of their lives, ambition, and family cause me to think of the brief time we have to leave our mark and to make our lives matter in some lasting way. Walking down the tree-lined path to the barns, cool winds blowing on our faces, sounds of rustling leaves, and the smell of the home lingering in my nostrils, I became a bit melancholy. A great life lived, a marriage of nearly sixty years, three daughters, a family farm, and now all that is left is the 240 acres of land and a million acres of sky. There is a daughter living a great distance away and a granddaughter living close by, but distant from the world of her gifted grandfather and family. That's all that is left except, of course, written words, and thousands of volumes that continue to inspire. Seasons change. Things change. Life changes, but hope is always reborn in the spring, and life moves on in meandering ways like a stream through rocks.

The thing to be remembered and cherished is the work of a gifted and disciplined man, a family that faced the challenges (and tragedy) of life and stayed together, leaving a legacy of love. This is strength to me, to my own, to my hope to live, love well, and to leave something that matters. And in the end, what matters most is a faithful family. As Sandberg said, "All the big people are simple, as simple as the unexplained wilderness. They love the universal things that are free to everybody. Light and air and food and love and some work are enough. In the varying phases of these cheap and common things, the great lives have found their joy."

As we walked back down the hill and away from the history of a family, I thought of the words that Alice shared when speaking of Big Daddy and his wife BeBe the day before, "Everybody was welcome at Mamma's house."

They were married for over fifty years, grubbing a livelihood through the Depression years, yet building a life where love was a given and could be trusted. Their life included the laughter of children echoing through the rooms or across the yard, where the fragrance of something good was always drifting from the kitchen stove, where the door was always open to family, friends, and strangers alike, and where the rockers on the front porch were used to watch the setting of the sun or children playing at dusk. Yes, the simple things of life make life worth living, and in an odd way, worth leaving.

This is the kind of family from which Alice found her values, garnered her strength to rise above the pieces of her broken dream, so she might give to me one like Freda, the love of my life. Freda gave me a strength beyond my own and left me two precious children and six grandchildren. I'm indebted, Alice, and I'm grateful.

Arriving back at Alice's house, I stopped by our home church, Hopeful Baptist. I walked to the front door of the old sanctuary. From these doors Freda and I emerged as husband and wife. The years passed so quickly, but with such adventure. The world was ours—literally. God so graced us. Now, though her body lies a few yards away, she is with the only One she ever loved more than me, and the One, of course, who loves her even more than I do. In that, I find solace.

As I look at the plaque by the door, I read, "Hopeful Baptist Church, organized August 7, 1887. This building erected 1948 . . ." and at the bottom, "Presented by R.P Dicks." That's Big Daddy. He is the one who walked Freda down the aisle, just inside those doors, and presented her to me. As I stood there, my heart crying out to relive that moment, I was reminded that the gift came from a family where "everybody was welcome at Mamma's." That included me. And since the moment it did, life has been better for me.

I'm glad Alice and I pilgrimaged together. Even today, if you look close enough, you can see the sadness in her eyes. And there is a quietness from being alone over the years, a fragility from past hurt, and a hesitation yet to risk much.

Though there is a quietness that comes from being alone, and a privacy that comes from a family culture, look closer and you will see a fierce strength. Look deeper still, and you will see a heart where "everybody is welcome at Mamma's."

Times have changed now. Things have changed—ways changed. We're in a time when we live in the present, giving little thought to our past, it seems, and perhaps even less to our future. Yet, as the Psalmist says, *"My times are in your hands"* (31:15). What was true for him is true for all of us. And so we pray, "God grant this heritage to our family—for generations to come."

Well, have I been "chasing Freda"? Maybe. And, if so, that's not all bad. It has led me to experience wonderful memories, to discover insights about myself and family, and is helping me become stronger and better prepared for the future.

This next step in my pilgrimage would become clearer and better defined at my next stop.

CHAPTER SEVEN
A Defining Time

West Florida
March 2010

I had finished speaking at the Baptist College of Florida. Under the strategic leadership of Dr. Thomas Kinchen, the school has become a strong educational institution. I had already planned to leave there and revisit the location where Freda and I had lived those first years of marriage. Our educational pursuits in science took us to the University of West Florida in Pensacola. We lived in Milton, just a few miles east of the university. We thought we would be there a couple of years. It ended up being six years, and we experienced some defining moments while there.

I have given a lot of thought to why I wanted to engage what I have come to refer to as *a pilgrimage of love*. For one thing, I wanted to recapture the experiences we shared—to relive those adventurous and exciting times. It was my hope to become stronger in the process, to help me remember the best of life together, to remove some of the fear of living without her, and to be able to share with our family in such a way that would empower us in our grief, as well as strengthen her legacy.

The decision to take this pilgrimage made it incumbent on me to decide how I would handle the emotional challenges. I decided I would:

- Trust God for His strength.
- Face my fears.
- Build my confidence.
- Believe the best for the future.
- Enjoy what I have.
- Live to make a difference.
- Let go of the difficult times and hold on to the good.

One of the questions I pondered long and hard was, "How

do I close the hole in my heart; that is, let go."

There was not a ready answer.

The night before leaving the school was restless for me. The excitement and anticipation kept me awake. The next morning the Tahoe purred steadily, rushing toward my destination. As I entered Milton, I was listening to *God's Sustaining Hand*, the CD Freda and the family had made a few years earlier after her remission. The song playing was "Open Door."

I entered Milton by Highway 90, stopping at the Black River where Freda and I had enjoyed friends and water sports. The emotional flood was like standing under a waterfall. The memory of those years came with force. Suddenly I was back in time and it seemed, for a moment, that Freda was present with me. But only for a moment, then the reality of her loss hit as a tidal wave. Not unexpected but, in fact, invited. How else could I and others profit from the loss?

Regaining my composure, I left the river to continue my journey, going past First Baptist Church of Milton, where Joe Bamberg served as senior pastor for almost fifty years. He was really the pastor of the community, often speaking at community events. He had also held many other places of leadership in the state of Florida. I can remember how honored I felt when he invited me, as a college student, to speak to the church family on a Sunday morning. Actually honored and intimidated—but very appreciative.

I stopped by Mt. Pleasant Baptist Church, where Freda and I served as Minister of Music/Youth for a while during college. George Kell was pastor, and he would, in time, become the man I referred to as my "father in the ministry." While there, I was listening to a song on the CD, "Hard to Get," sung by our son John. I remember how it seemed that God was *hard to get* during our time in Milton when I struggled to understand His call into ministry—and now *hard to get* as I tried to make sense of the suffering and loss of my wife. That being said, I am convinced that God is more willing to reveal himself than we are willing to understand—or capable of comprehending.

I stopped by Pine Terrace Baptist Church. Once a mission, it was now a large and flourishing church. Here Freda sang at the wedding of Greg Kell, who was a student of hers and the son of George Kell. He was a bright kid then, now an effective pastor in one of the fastest growing churches in our state.

Then to Chumuckla, where I pastored my first little rural church. Our children were just babies. The experience was a boot camp spiritual experience, yet I still have good friends who live there. I will never forget that my grandparents, who meant so much to me, surprised me with their presence at my ordination service. What an unexpected joy!

The visit with Martin and Martha Salter was special. They played a pivotal role in our move to Texas to attend Southwestern Seminary. Across the years and the miles, they have remained supportive and loyal—a rare jewel on the ring of friendship.

From there to visit the first home that Freda and I built—that is a story in itself. I couldn't find the location, so I stopped by to visit with Doris Kell, wife of the late George Kell. She spoke kindly of Freda, saying, "She was a saint." With her guidance I found 6276 Glendale Drive. I sat in front of the home where we first lived with our children. What memories! Talk about feeling homesick!

And I wanted to visit the hospitals where our children were born. Christa was born in the Baptist Hospital in Pensacola. It's interesting that, as I arrived, I was listening to Freda and Christa, now 34, sing "Amazing Grace" together. That brought a smile to my face. Then I drove to where our son John was born—West Florida Hospital. This time I was listening to "He's Been Faithful to Me." And I realized afresh, indeed He has been.

Next was my visit to the University of West Florida, our alma mater. It has a beautiful 1,000 acre campus, which has changed so much that I needed to go to the Welcome Center for a map! As I parked and began my walk, I had butterflies in my stomach. First, the commons building, where Freda and I sometimes enjoyed lunch and coffee, then the science building, where Freda and I had taken a zoology class and others. Then to the conference room where I had met with faculty members to interview for dental school. It was that day, in that room, that I understood God's call to vocational ministry—yes, another story. Then on the nature trail where Freda and I had strolled between classes, I paused to reflect, and wrote:

I can't believe you are gone. Sometimes I wish we could have gone together. But that would only have been selfish. Now I must travel without you— but I do have those you left me. I leave this place (sacred in memory), this place of beginnings, with gratitude. Listening to "More Than Wonderful," which speaks of "beyond my highest hopes and fondest dreams," I have to say that statement captured my experience with you. Forty years—so long, yet, they passed so quickly. Who would have thought our journey together would end so soon— yet be so full?

I had a lunch appointment with Otha and May Grant, now ages eighty-two and eight-one respectively. They too, have remained such good friends for so long. Then by Santa Rosa Hospital where Dr. Watson, surgeon, completed a successful surgery on Freda not long after our marriage.

I left West Florida, having completed my objective. The song, "Walk on Through the Door to a Greater Power You've Ever Known Before," was playing and I was thinking: *That's hard for me to believe. How can I be stronger without her than with her? No way, except for the "fresh anointing" which the song speaks of.* He's "inviting you to walk where you've never walked before," says another phrase of the song. *That* would be true. Somehow, I think that is the message from Freda to me as well.

Maybe that was why I went there—for this truth to come home to me. And what does this mean to me, even today?
- I will move forward with a new strength gained.
- There *is* an open door before me—I must walk through it.

- I *will* have a new and fresh anointing—a power never known before.
- Don't quit now—develop a strategy for the future—"Stand on my own."

It also means that I must face my fears. What are they?

- That I can make only a limited contribution without her.
- That I won't be able to capture and communicate the pain of grief in such a way that it will matter and be helpful to others.
- That I don't know the long-term impact on family.
- That I won't understand what it means to "let go."
- That I won't finish well—as she did.

These are some of the fears that come my way—especially in the dark of the night. But the Spirit God gave us does not make us timid, but gives us power, love, and self-discipline (see 2 Timothy 1:7). And one thing Jesus repeatedly said was, "Don't be afraid." Fear is an enemy. It must be defeated early on. As Emerson stated, "Do the things you fear, and the death of fear is certain."

So, my next step toward growth and change did become clearer to me. Having identified my specific fears, I could address them head on. Accepting the fact that there was an open door, wanted or not, and acknowledging the affirmation of a new and fresh strength, I could begin thinking more strategically about the future.

Our fears are some of the things that rob us of a bright future. They are a prison cell that locks us within its confines, a powerful force that constricts our faith and abilities, that undercuts our confidence. If we can unmask them, that in itself removes much of their power. This frees us to move through doors open to us and begin to rebuild our lives. We need to do this because, as you read the next pages, you will see the need for courage.

CHAPTER EIGHT
A Hot Day in the Amazon Basin

Brazil

June 2010

In 2002 my son John, a friend Joe Fincher, and I had gone to northern Brazil to coordinate a mission partnership in Boa Vista. We made a side trip into the West Amazon basin to catch some Peacock bass. I had a strong interest in the villages of the basin and bringing the hope of Christ to the Ribeirinhos people. Once in a village and among the people, my heart had been captured. Now, nine years later, the vision has become Amazon Vision Ministries, a work that brings medical, dental, humanitarian, and educational care along with the hope of Christ to the people of the basin. We have seen literally thousands come to Christ, and the adventure would yield a book of its own. This work is now managed by a Board of Directors to whom I am very grateful.

Prior to this work in the Amazon basin, was the work in Boa Vista. Actually, it was Freda who led the first team there in 1993. Her heart was captured by Brazil and, though she was unable to go into the basin, the work was her passion. Now on this trip to the basin, my son John and grandson Cade were with me, along with other team members.

One of the difficult things for me has been dealing with Freda's clothes. Now, seven months after her loss, I needed to make some final decisions. Yes, I had been in her closet many times after her death. Sometimes I stood and just stared at her clothes, relating particular clothes with specific experiences. Sometimes I put my arms around a certain dress or sweater, hoping for her scent to bring her back into my presence. Sometimes I would just hold them close to my chest and weep for her memory; other times I would see an outfit that prompted a funny memory and laugh out loud.

The time came when I knew I was ready to part with some

of her clothes. With the help of my daughter Christa and my daughter-in-law Tina, I made some hard decisions. Some of her clothing I have kept, like her wedding dress. I gave some special items to family and a few to her friends. I gave some to persons in need, some to a consignment boutique, some were buried at a sacred place, and still others I carried with me to Brazil. Every item that left her closet did so for a particular reason, just as those that remain do so for a particular purpose. My journal entry explains the experience in Brazil.

For some of her clothing to be in Brazil seemed right—her heart was so set on the people there. So I chose the clothing most suitable, packed them up, and now they are with me.

Today I made arrangements with Pastor Naton to enlist the help of Maria Hymurda to distribute the clothing to the villages. I had brought them 2,000 miles, thinking it was fitting to leave some of her clothing among the people. She was with the first mission team in Brazil and had left her love imprinted upon the spiritual landscape of the country.

Now, sitting in the cabin on the boat, looking at the clothing, I found it difficult to let them go. I wanted them back. No, I wanted her back.

One of her shirts lying on top that I loved to see her wear took me back in time, way back to our beginning. Now I am looking at the ending. Where, pray tell, did the years go? This I know, the years were not spent—but were rather invested—some of them here in this village. This is where Freda's clothes, with their memories, belong and where they shall stay. I took the clothes ashore. People within the village wear them now.

Having completed our trip and heading back toward civilization, we each thought of family back home, and they bore deeply on our minds. When,

within signal range, John called his wife Tina;
I listened from a distance. Though I couldn't and
didn't want to understand what was being said
(I considered it private), I could discern the excited
tone being communicated to the one he loves most.

All of a sudden it dawned on me afresh; I had no
one to call. Oh yes, I had family and friends whom
I could call—but not Freda. A painful moment. But
why wouldn't it be?

The sunset was beautiful. Freda would have
loved it. Somehow, in the mysterious but loving
ways of God, I felt her reflected in the sunset.

Late in the evening, with team members sitting
in a circle on the top deck of the boat, I shared
the poem that I had written late one night in my
cabin—"When She Came into View"—(the one that
you read earlier). It was a moment to honor her, to
love her in a tangible way.

The work of love in Brazil continues. She will
always be a part of it.

Things such as dealing with the clothes of a
loved one seem like such a small thing. Yet, in the
process of grief, it is not. It is significant in the pro-
cess of healing. And, in this case, a part of a shared
vision and ministry.

As you move through your grief, there will be many practical
matters to deal with. Some of them may spark a bit of fear or
maybe paralyzing fear within you. Involving family and making intentional decisions can help you overcome fear and build
confidence in your competence to make good choices, make
good memories, and make a contribution in the process. These
considerations are important because there will be on-going
decisions to be made. How you make them will not only affect
your life, but those around you as well. This truth came home
to me, even more at my next stop . . .

CHAPTER NINE
The Cool Island Winds

July 24, 2010

Elizabeth Point, the beach house on Amelia Island, is where we spent our last anniversary together—now almost a year ago at this writing. Although her health issues had become very difficult, it was a beautiful weekend together. Today, I relive those memories.

As I sat in front of the historic home, I put on the song, "This Guy's In Love With You" by Herb Alpert. The freshness, excitement, and unbelievability of our first love swept over me. As Herb Alpert sings in his song, " . . . my hands were shaking" on those first encounters with Freda. She was known for her intellect; she was popular on campus as a personality; and her standards were known to be high for her relationships. Yes, it was unbelievable that she would take an interest in me. I felt if I had her in my life, all of life would be good—and it has been, even in the midst of our greatest challenges. As the song says, "My heart keeps breaking because I need your love—I want your love." And as another song says, "I don't know if I will get over you. I don't know if I want to." How can I get over her and why would I? How can anyone get over real love? With her I discovered the meaning of love. I knew the best of life. How do you get over oneness? What does it mean, anyway, to get over someone?

If it means to move on with life and other relationships as if this one never existed, then I deem that impossible with the experience of real love. If it means to learn how to protect memories and to nurture the continued influence of such a life well lived, then I deem that possible. If it means to use that love as inspiration to continue to live with passion and to motivate one to pursue a path of love, then I deem that possible. If it means to continue a legacy, to perhaps one day find someone who understands the *meaning* of such loss and share love with that person, then I deem that possible. Perhaps desirable, but not a given. Yes, "this guy's in love with you"—still. And always will be. I still have her love and will for all eternity. The hope is that her love will continue to empower me to love family and friends more deeply and more consistently than ever.

I walked down to the place where we last walked on the beach together. The walk took all the physical strength she had, but then that is what she always gave—the best she had. We stood right there, the wind blowing in her hair, that beautiful smile on her face as the setting sun cast its ebbing glow upon her. Now I stand alone, except for a strong sense of her presence.

The beaches, on both coasts, are the places of many memories. My mind drifts to the good times with our children on the beaches of Florida. I especially remember the first time Freda saw the Pacific, running to get her feet in the cold waters like a little girl who was seeing the ocean for the first time. Then there was the memory of the beach in Oregon just two years ago. We always wanted to ride horses on the beach, and finally the dream came true in Oregon. The morning was cold, and there was a fine mist in the air, yet she rode with exuberance.

Now I stand here wishing there was opportunity to create more memories. There's not, but I cherish the memories of her love of life and how it taught me to live.

I returned to the Elizabeth Point Lodge. I took the elevator to the third floor, room ten, where we last stayed. The room was small but cozy. It was a night of, well, restful love.

Going to the porch on the second floor, I sat in one of the two rockers we sat in. As I rocked and reflected, I thought of what one of my friends said to me in a text message. "What I realized is you are more married to Freda now than you have ever been." There is a sense in which her love has captured my heart and gripped my soul as never before. Maybe that's because I understand better now what in life and love is real and what is not.

I left Elizabeth Point to go to the historic district of

Amelia Island where she and I walked and talked. After lunch at O'Kane's, an Irish pub, I walked into one shop after another that we had enjoyed together—clothing shops like the Gauzeway, which had styles that fit her so well; the Pineapple Patch, where a young lady had on an elegant purple dress that would have looked so good on Freda; Tiger Palens, with lots of white which I loved to see on her. I always wanted to buy her cool clothing. She was always looking for the "simple and elegant" and "the good buy."

I stepped into the "Christmas on the River" store. This brought a smile to my face. Freda was a Christmas girl. She loved the celebration of her faith, the keeping and building of family traditions, and finding gifts that were particularly suited for her loved ones. She will always adorn Christmas in our family.

Then the shop which held a special moment this last year, Celtic Charm. I remembered how we were browsing. I was listening to Celtic music and watching her. She walked over to me, and I expressed my concern for her health and healing. With a soft smile and a gentleness of tone, she made a simple reply. "Let it go. Either way, I will be okay." Well, she is now okay. She is *far better* as the apostle would put it. I will let "it" go, that is, the pain of her suffering, of seeing her suffer. But I will not let go of her. She was God's gift to me—a gift to be kept for all time.

I thought of the poem that was given to me by a friend. The words are these:

MISS ME, BUT LET ME GO
When I have come to the end of the road
And the sun has set for me,
I want no rites in a gloom-filled room,
Why cry for a soul set free?
Miss me a little, but not too much,
And not with your head bowed low.

Remember the love that we once shared . . .
Miss me . . . but let me go.
For this is a journey we all must take
And one must go alone.
It's all part of the Master's Plan . . .
A step on the road to home.
So when you are sad and sick of heart
Go to the friends we know . . .
And bury your sorrows in serving our Lord.
Miss me . . . but let me . . . go.
—Anonymous

I see her positive attitude, her courage, and her wisdom in the words of the poem. And I progressively will be released from the pain—but not from her. If the meaning is similar to getting over her and if that means to find the inspiration in her love to move on and embrace life and love, then okay. Otherwise, how foolish to let go of the best of my life.

On the way back to the Tahoe, a stop by Le Clos, the French restaurant where we enjoyed a warm, cozy environment, good food, and a sweet time of sharing.

I was so eager to get to Amelia Island to remember all this, then so reluctant to leave. Memories were so vivid, her presence so strong. That day my heart was played like an instrument on the chords of memory. I had been reminded that each time she put her hand to the keyboard, she made beautiful music—beautiful life. I went home, not because I wanted to leave this place of companionship, but because I knew I must—love and legacy demand it.

Driving home, I listened to music we both enjoyed. When I arrived, I was listening to pianist Jim Brickman, the song, "Bittersweet." While I had wept on and off all day, now, driving up to our home, I wept uncontrollably. Why? It's hard to say. The emotional engagement of the day, the beautiful life she gave me, the dreams she had helped to come true, and the home she herself had designed that the Lord allowed us to enjoy together for three years before she went to be with Him. It's a place of simple beauty, a place of quiet peace, and what I refer to as a place of "creative life" and laughter—a hub of love. The tears reflected healthy grief, I think, a deep gratitude, and the celebration of joy. In fact, the question may be raised, "Is this grief or celebration?" or is it "Grief and celebration"? The latter, I think. Love always gives reason to celebrate.

I received a message from a good friend today. Daniel Morris, a young man of unusual maturity for his age and gifted in his work, wrote concerning my pilgrimage, "Gary, what you are doing is good! I'm so sorry for the pain you feel, but celebrate Freda's life with you! Your journey through this difficult time has been a learning time for me. Your passion and love for Freda and your family has brought my own relationship (with my family) to a deeper level of love and appreciation. Freda's life and your loss are not in vain. I hope you know that."

These words were refreshing, like rain on parched ground. Perhaps more importantly, they were encouraging. Encouraging that her influence continues and that my intentional engagement of grief is helpful to others in their journey of love. Hopefully your journey with grief is included.

One of the things we deal with in our grief is—what does it mean to let go, to move on? That question should be asked, but it is hard to answer. In fact, it can't be answered on the front side of our grief. If we conclude that it means to put away the past, to look to someone else to meet our needs (before we ever understand what they really are), then we have drawn a wrong conclusion, and that will spell trouble in time.

If we come to understand these phases to mean we must work through the stages of our grief, we must learn from our grief, we must nurture our best memories, we must grow through the process, then we will, in time, regain our footing and experience health again. Make no mistake. This is an important question to raise, and critically important to answer correctly. Why? As I said in the previous chapter, because it will affect our own quality of life, our future, and will impact those around us for good or ill.

These decisions are guided by our faith, or should be. My next visit would be to a place where my faith was greatly strengthened.

CHAPTER TEN
A Spiritual and Academic Pursuit

Texas
October 3, 2010

Our time in Texas clarified God's call to me to vocational ministry. We spent five years there as I worked on my Master's and Doctorate degrees at Southwestern Baptist Theological Seminary. The academics were challenging and fulfilling. The ministry experience was boot camp in type, but set a foundation and direction for my ministry.

We made friends—life-long friends in Texas. They marked our lives. In returning to revisit, memories of Freda's and my time there, my daughter Christa made this trip with me. I'm glad she did. She and our son John spent their first five years in Texas. They loved friends there like family and still do. And it was special to me for her to be with me. We enjoy a great relationship, and I found strength in her presence.

Jarrod and Megan Reed, a young couple God had called to vocational ministry, were also with me. They wanted to visit Southwestern Seminary as a possibility for further education. They are gifted, fun, and a joy to have along. I am convinced they will be a conduit of good in the lives of many in the years to come.

Christa and I stayed in the home of Gary and Ann Fisher. They have been unswerving friends since we first met. Other friends came to join us, including Dorothy Knowles, now ninety years of age. She and her husband, Bob, were the Texas "grandparents" for Christa and John. She is still feisty and much loved. What a joy to spend time with these friends, share memories, and reflect.

I retraced all the important places in Godly, Texas, where I pastored First Baptist Church for almost five years. Each place had its own significance and message. Then I returned to the campus of Southwestern, the student center, where I had spent so much time studying, the classrooms where I studied Greek, History, Hebrew, Hermeneutics, and other courses of study.

Four things gripped me. One, the Rotunda with the portraits of past presidents of the Seminary, men of great wisdom and faith. I want my life to count for the Kingdom as theirs did. Second, the memory of standing in the hallway years ago talking with Dr. L. L. Collins. He made a statement in that brief conversation that served as a guide and caution to this day. He said, "One of the greatest dangers in ministry is for the sacred to become familiar." How true I have discovered that to be.

Third, when under the tutelage of Dr. Jack McGorman, Professor of New Testament and Greek, he shared this truth: "If you have more truth on your lips than grace in your heart, you will do damage to the cause of Christ and the hearts of others." That statement was about communicating truth in love, a valuable insight that has been a guide for my life.

Fourth, I went to the chapel. I remember times of morning worship, of significant decisions that I made, and of moments of inspiration that have lasted to this day. The chapel was empty, except for an organist rehearsing. I dropped to my knees and thanked God for the opportunity to have been there and for Freda. Without her, I wouldn't have made it through. This graduate institution, the largest of its kind in the world, is a sacred place for me. Men and women of faith touched and shaped my life. My faith was strengthened. I have been forever grateful.

The visit was difficult at times, but for the most part, a real encouragement. Our years there were full of adventure, challenge, and reward. Today, thirty years later, I know just how much.

CHAPTER ELEVEN
The Place of Life and Loss

Little Rock
November 2010

Little Rock—the final stop you may say. Rene, the younger of my two sisters, had decided to go with me. Why? For one reason, she loved Freda. Freda had loved Rene well in her early, formative years, and she had led her to Christ. Rene felt an emotional and spiritual bond. And I think she wanted to be with me to provide support in any way possible. I was glad to have her along.

Then there was Adam Palmer, a young writer from Tulsa, Oklahoma. We had a shared interest in the life story of Freda, and he had come to Gainesville to interview about twenty-five family members and friends about her life. At the end of those interviews he commented, "She seemed to have a way of attracting special people." That she did! Adam had traveled with us to speak to physicians and friends who knew her in Little Rock.

There, where she died, were a lot of mixed emotions, of course—a mixture of anticipation and dread. The bittersweet as always. This was something I didn't want to do but needed to do. Her loss, when it happened, came quickly on that appointed day. And by days end, my son and I were leaving Little Rock, headed back to Gainesville without her.

Having left abruptly, I wanted and needed to go back to say thank you to the people who had become special to us and who were so supportive and helpful. And another reason I needed to return was to open this closet door of my heart, clean it out, and close it with peace of mind. This trip proved to be a good decision.

Arriving at the airport in Little Rock, the sights and the scenes were so familiar. Memories flooded my mind and tears, my eyes. I noticed that I kept looking around, thinking each time I would see her standing there. I knew, of course, this would not happen. Yet, I was swayed to think so. I wanted to fall to my knees and wail in sorrow, but I couldn't in the presence of my sister. It would be hard for her to see that, and embarrassing to me.

My stomach churned and my soul as well. Ten years of traveling here for her treatments and tests—the emotional ups and downs of her health at a given time, the hopes, the disappointments, the fears, the anxieties—they all came back with force, and my heart was swept into chaos. Yet, in a strange way, I was called back to this place of her care and her loss, while at the same time everything within me wanted to run away—but I didn't.

The next day (Friday the 19th) we had breakfast with Bobbie Lowery. She and her husband Tom had given us a special place in their hearts and home. Over the years, they had become like family. Then Rene, Adam, and I left for the Little Rock Cancer Research Center. I stopped by the community bakery as Freda and I often did at her initiative. She would take pastries to the medical staff. That was one way Freda expressed her appreciation to those who cared for her. The week before, on the anniversary of her death, I had sent flowers to the medical faculty and staff as another expression of our gratitude.

We had an appointment with Dr. Van Rhea, her last primary care physician. The first thing he said to me was, "I loved her." The second thing, "She was a delightful and brave woman." The third thing, "Thank you for the roses. I've never had someone say 'thank you' a year later. We are grateful for your expression of gratitude."

I listened as Adam asked Dr. Van Rhea one question after another. Dr. Van Rhea spoke of a cure for multiple myeloma with the less aggressive gene. That was the first time that word "cure" had ever been used in reference to this disease. Then he noted, " . . . and Freda was a part of seeing that happen." He was referring to her willingness to engage experimental protocols. I smiled as I thought to myself, *Yes, that was Freda.*

After we finished our interview, the three of us walked across to the building where so much of her treatment had taken place and where I ultimately lost her. Rene and Adam kept a distance, giving me some space and privacy. I walked over to the place where she had stood for the last time. As sick as she was, she looked at the cloudless sky, broke into that beautiful smile, and said, "What a beautiful morning." Then she sat in her wheelchair and entered the center as a fighter enters the ring. Minutes later she was with the Lord. As I stood there remembering with clarity her words, her face, her courage, I wept uncontrollably.

I entered the building and stood in the exact spot where she had left to meet Christ. The thought came to my mind, "The disease finally took her body, but not her life. She lives on. Her pilgrimage is over. She is at home. The old has gone—the new has come."

Anita Carlton, receptionist and assistant, saw us in the lobby. She ran out with a smile on her face, exclaiming, "Can it be you? I wanted to tell you one more time, how much I loved Freda. When she came, we didn't take care of her, she took care of us." I understood what she was saying.

My business at the Center was done. I knew in my heart it was done—closure had occurred. The heart had not been healed, but my mind found peace. I left there to visit special places in and around Little Rock. For example, Freda and I had spent much time at a Barnes and Noble bookstore between her appointments. We would read, talk, and plan; I would study because I often flew back and forth to keep my leadership responsibilities at Westside.

The Beanery, on the outskirts of Little Rock, was another place of good food, coffee, rest, and reflection. The three of us had lunch there as I shared memories with Rene and Adam.

Then to Marbell Park, beautifully situated along the Arkansas River. We had come here many times to the place of vibrant green in summer and to bright, multi-colors in the fall; we walked, talked, prayed, and looked for strength for the next day. It was a beautiful place of refuge for us both.

As we stood under a large pine, the breeze blowing across our faces and the sound of water running behind us, I observed, "You know, given her circumstances, she could have made my life a hell, but instead she turned it into an opportunity for growth, accomplishment, love, and sweet memories."

No trip here would be complete without a stop by the big mall, the Park Plaza. We often stopped there for Freda to walk after having a bone marrow biopsy. It was important for her to walk to diminish the pain and quicken the healing. I walked through our favorite stores and reminisced about some of our special shopping times—often shopping for family and friends.

After an affectionate goodbye to our friends, we left Little Rock. It was done. I had returned, I worked (emotionally), I wept, I wrapped my heart around as many good memories and as much significance as possible. What an incalculable gift God gave me in her! To let go, whatever "let go" means, feels like letting go of my last, best hope in life. I would go back home to continue to build what we started and to dream new dreams.

Will I go back to Little Rock? Maybe. Probably. But never again for the same reason. It's done. But friends remain . . .

I did my best to pen a poem that day to express the feelings within my heart:

The Day She Was Born
Conceived in love,
Born in pain,
A pretty little girl was given for my gain.
Her hair was thick and black,
Her eyes were beautiful brown,
Her mind was quick,
Her heart was tender.
Cradled in family,
Nurtured in faith,

An attractive young lady she became.
We stood at the altar,
She was mine,
We looked to the future,
It was our time.
Life together we lived with passion,
Full of purpose, full of love,
Life passed so quickly,
Now our time is done,
Yet you remain mine—for all time.

The day Freda was born she was a gift to me and to all who knew her. Freda's mom, Alice, worked while pregnant with Freda. Her father had already left the family. Alice worked through eight months of pregnancy. When the time arrived, she labored until 10:00 p.m. when Freda was delivered by Dr. L.J. Arnold, Jr. Alice left the hospital at 8:00 a.m. the next morning to go to stay with Big Daddy and BeBe, Freda's grandparents. They would shape her life for years to come. The day she was born, she entered their home to be nurtured in love and faith. Though I was born a month earlier, in the same hospital, and delivered by the same doctor, I wouldn't know until twenty-one years later that the day she was born, my destiny was set—and for my good.

I had decided before my journey began, the questions that needed to be answered. Here are some of them:

- Why do I grieve so deeply? Answer: She was my soul mate.
- Why have I struggled so with her loss? Answer: Her suffering was so long, seemed so unfair, and in the end, her life cut short.
- Why am I angry? Answer: I'm not. Somehow, in God's grace, I never dealt with anger against God or life. One reason why is explained in "Bow the Knee," a song Freda loved to sing. The song says:

There are moments on our journey following the Lord
where God illumines every step we take.

There are times when circumstances
make perfect sense to us,
as we try to understand each move He makes.

When the path grows dim
and our questions have no answers,
turn to Him.

There are days when clouds surround us and the rain
begins to fall,
the cold and lonely winds won't cease to blow.

And there seems to be no reason for the suffering we feel;
We are tempted to believe God does not know.

When the storms arise,
don't forget we live by faith and not by sight.
Bow the knee.

Trust the heart of your Father
when the answer goes beyond what you can see,
Bow the knee.

Lift your eyes toward heaven
and believe the One who holds eternity.
And when you don't understand the purpose of His plan,
In the presence of the King,
Bow the knee.

I remember when Freda was first diagnosed. I felt hurt. I felt abandoned. I felt exposed—but not angry. And, of course, Freda didn't feel angry. She didn't even feel the hurt that I did. That confidence came from her strong and simple—not simplistic—faith. And we both, in the end, sought to live out the premise, " . . . when you don't understand the purpose of His plan—bow the knee." When we do this, when we trust the heart of the Father, we may still experience the full range of human emotion, but we don't get stuck in the quicksand of anger.

• Why am I afraid? Answer: Because all of my adult life she has been by my side.

- Why do I lack motivation, even though I continue to perform with a high standard? Answer: Everything looks black and white because the color of her love is gone.
- Is guilt a factor? Answer: I don't think so. At least not any more than that stage of grief. In the end love, forgiveness, and commitment won.
- What am I going to do? Answer: What I should do. Celebrate her love, find direction, build on legacy, and love the family she left me.
- How do I do this? Answer: Focus on the good, face my fear, get started.

My journal entry made as I was leaving Little Rock:

> Sweetheart, I don't want to let you go. I don't want to do life without you. I don't have a choice. To honor you, to love you, to love what you love, I must move on in His strength and yours. I know you would want for me what I would want for you— love, health, hope, fulfillment, peace, excitement, freedom, joy, growth, change, passion, and hard work. These I will pursue.

Yes, faith—a vital, practical, transcendent faith within my heart—was revealed. Men and women of faith who have loved me and taught me not only marked my life, they helped me find my own. In the most difficult times of life, and in our greatest moments of opportunity, there is no substitute for an authentic faith and relationship with Jesus Christ, who faced the full gamut of human emotion, and gives to us His love, strength, and guidance as we encounter our own. It was Freda's faith that took a hellish experience and turned it into an opportunity of growth, accomplishment, love, and sweet memories. The same can be true for you.

Two more stops on the winding pilgrimage will prove helpful. The next stop took me to the heart of our country and to a special place within my heart.

CHAPTER TWELVE

The Heartbeat of Our Nation

Washington
May 25, 2011

In May 2009, Freda and I were invited by the Family Research Council to attend a Summit Meeting in Washington, D.C. The meeting involved congressmen, pastors, and other leaders from across the country. We were both pleased to have the invitation and accepted. This arena represents one area of my concern and ministry.

Freda was not doing so well, but felt she could make the trip. We left for D.C. with excitement. I looked forward to such a forum, to the meetings set with our congressmen, and most of all to a few days with Freda in the heartbeat of our nation.

We were informed during the meetings, inspired as we reviewed again the irrefutable evidence of our Christian heritage, and intrigued by our discussion with the congressmen. We particularly enjoyed lunch at an Irish pub and dinner at a small, quaint Italian restaurant. Although Freda was challenged physically in walking to our destinations on Capitol Hill, we made some wonderful memories and came home better prepared in our leadership.

When the invitation came again in 2011, I was willing and able to accept and for the same reasons I went in 2009. Of course, Freda wasn't with me this time, but I would have the opportunity to retrace our steps and relive some memories. I was eager to go.

When I arrived at the capital city, scenes and memories were fresh. It felt strange without her. As I moved through one meeting, then another, I remembered conversations and insights that we shared. I cherished the remembrances.

I returned to the Irish restaurant, Dubliner's Pub, for lunch, sat at the same table, and ordered the same food. Then, one evening I wanted to return to the Italian restaurant that we had enjoyed so much. Oddly enough, I couldn't remember the name or location. Asking the concierge at the hotel proved unhelpful. Looking at the Italian restaurants in the vicinity, I settled on one that I thought must be right. A taxi drive there, and I discovered it wasn't, so back to my list. I wasn't going to give up. This memory was important to me.

Now with names and addresses in hand, along with the GPS on my phone, I chose one restaurant, then another, to no avail. Okay, now after almost two hours of walking, sweating, and running out of options, I was about to give up. Then I looked up and noticed a familiar street. This was the street! I walked hurriedly in the direction where I thought the restaurant to be. Soon I was standing in front of it—the Bistro Italiano, 320 D Street NE. I stood there with tears in my eyes, having finally found it. Yes, I was taking pictures. Two couples sat at the table in the bay window at the front. By now they were staring at me wondering what this strange man was doing standing in front of the restaurant, crying and taking pictures. Nonetheless, I went inside chagrined that they were at *our* table.

Seated, I enjoyed the delicious Italian cuisine again. But most of all, I enjoyed the memories and the satisfaction of having found, at last, this special place.

When Freda and I were there together, as mentioned, she had trouble navigating the hills around the Capitol. We didn't know it then, but would discover later, that this was because the myeloma had invaded her heart and created dysfunction.

But I remember vividly on the day we had an appointment with Congressman Cliff Stearns, we would walk a while, then she needed to rest. I encouraged her to allow me to call and reschedule the meeting. Her answer, of course, was "No." That was just another expression of her resolve. We made the meeting and benefited from our time with the congressman and others on his staff.

So then, how could I not show resolve in finding the places we had visited together—the places I could again sense her presence and see her tender smile?

Resolve. That virtue can be hard to come by. Resolve is usually in proportion to the depth of our convictions and our sense of purpose. Our resolve is strengthened as we see it in the lives of others—especially those closest to us.

In traveling the road of recovery, you will need to call upon resolve again and again. With it, you will arrive at the destination of health. Find those persons in your life who model resolve; draw on their strength at your weakest moments. I, too, would need a special portion of resolve at my final stop.

CHAPTER THIRTEEN
A University Dorm

Tallahassee
May 29, 2011

It had been on my mind since her death. The trip back to Tallahassee where she attended Florida State University was to be part of my pilgrimage of grief and recovery. Due to a demanding schedule in my work and family, the trip was delayed. I wanted to go back to the dorm where she stayed during her first year there while I was still at the college in Lake City.

Problem was, I didn't know which dorm. I had letters from her that she wrote while there. I was hoping to pull them out and get the address off the envelope. Surprise! There was a box number only. But I was resolved. So off I went.

I took the route we traveled then: 1969-1970. It was Highway 90. I had forgotten how beautiful the drive is between Lake City and Tallahassee. As I traveled, sipping on one of my staples of life—coffee—and listening to love songs we had enjoyed, I relived, one memory after another prompted by familiar sites.

Two hours later I arrived at the campus of the university. Wow, so much had changed over forty years. I stopped at a hotel to get a general sense of where the dorms might be. But that was not much help. Driving onto campus, I stopped one person and then another with little information gained. Finally, I found someone who gave me the vicinity. I walked to one building and then the next. When, about to give up, I found myself standing in a parking lot in front of a dorm where I had parked an hour earlier. But it was coed; her dorm was not—then. But her presence seemed so strong. I said to myself, *This is it*. I was standing in front of Cawthon Hall.

I pulled out the box of her letters and chose the first one at hand. In that letter she had written about her dorm—Cawthon Hall. I had stumbled upon it, or was it answered prayer—since I had asked for His help!

I had parked where we parked. I was standing looking at the dorm doors I had walked anxiously toward to see her. My stomach seemed to be full of butterflies. My heart raced and my breath, at moments, seemed to be taken away.

I began reading one letter with a thirst for the next, like a drama unfolding—but one that had already been lived. I read the words on the page, but I seemed to hear her voice as if she were reading the words to me.

As I read, I was overwhelmed by her insight into love, her expression of love for me, her commitment to love Christ while here on this campus. In fact, she said in the letter that she would soon move to Sally Hall to get away from the party girls who were her roommates, ones "I would not want her with." She had exhausted her efforts to share Christ and common sense with them.

In one letter dated September of 1969, she was lamenting us not being together on my birthday and wrote, "I hope we can spend the rest of our birthdays together." We did! Just not enough of them.

As I read her words, I longed to hold her in my arms as I did in saying good night or goodbye when I returned to Lake City. How tender her heart. How warm her embrace. I reached for the Shalimar I had brought and sprayed a mist on my hand. That fragrance was uniquely hers. She wore it then, and it remained a favorite over the years. Waves of euphoria and grief washed across me, leaving both the soul and body like the grains of sand on the seashore—awash. Yet, as the tidal wave of memories of her love crashed across my heart, my spirit caught breath for life again, but the body was weakened to the knees. Such would the day be—again and again.

I pray—"Thank you, Lord, for the *'wife of my youth.'*" She was the perfect gift to me. I wish I had been more for her much sooner. She knew so much more about love. She had so much more strength to give love. I have sought your forgiveness, Lord, and found it. I rest in your love and grace—and hers. Yet, that same love compels me to regret that I did not, could not, love more and better from the beginning. But Lord, in the end our love saw us through—we finished—we finished well. She left the imprint of her love across my life and around the world, the same love she expressed in this letter that I hold in my hand. "Thank you, Lord, for your gift to me. May that love help me to live well and love well now, without her."

I reached for my Bible. I had set it on the hood of the Tahoe along with letters and the Shalimar. The Lord directed me to Psalm 90. How fitting.

> *Lord, you have been our dwelling place*
> *throughout all generations . . .*
> *For a thousand years in your sight*
> *are like a day that has just gone by,*
> *or like a watch in the night . . .*
> *The length of our days is seventy years—*
> *or eighty, if we have the strength;*
> *Teach us to number our days aright,*
> *that we may gain a heart of wisdom. . .*
> *May your deeds be shown to your servants,*
> *your splendor to their children.*
> *May the favor of the Lord our God rest upon us;*
> *establish the work of our hands for us—*
> *yes, establish the work of our hands.*

And in Psalm 91:

> *"Because he loves me," says the Lord, "I will rescue him;*
> *I will protect him, for he acknowledges my name.*
> *He will call on me, and I will answer him;*
> *I will be with him in trouble,*
> *I will deliver him and honor him."*

Lord, you did establish the work of our hands—and that work remains. Now, Lord establish the work of my hands; no, it will always be "our" hands because of her influence and strength in my life. Place me in the center of that call that yet burns in my heart and in keeping with Your promise.

I was so torn to leave. (I say this every time, I know.) To leave that spot seemed to leave her. How could I move?

I was paralyzed. I lifted my hand, the hand with Shalimar, to my face and smelled the fragrance. In that moment, and for only a fleeting moment, I felt her embrace. The embrace of a good night kiss and goodbye—till next time we would be together.

She used to sing "Until Then," one of her favorite songs of faith:

> *Heartaches here are but stepping stones.*
> *This troubled world is not my final home.*
> *Until then my heart will go on singing, until then*
> *with joy I will carry on.*

May it be so!

One other place was on my mind, Shady Sea Baptist Church in Crawfordville. We had helped Pastor Ovid Lewis (former pastor of our home church) at this little church during the three months we were both at Florida State University. It was, you might say, the beginning of my ministry, the ministry I didn't know I would have—not having understood my call to ministry at the time.

Like the dorm, it was difficult to find. I asked residents in the area without success. Then, stopping to speak to a young man selling melons, I got the information I needed: 47 Shady Sea Street. I found the church. Well kept, but not so different from forty years ago. There were many children then and not many adults. Freda and I drove forty-five minutes each week to help this little band of believers. Now I sat listening to her sing on her CD "Touch Through Me," and yes, since then His love has touched many through her.

I remembered Wilmer and Hanna Dykes, pillars of the church. They lived in the house just across the street. I remembered their warm hospitality. "We never lock our doors," he said. "We want everyone to always feel welcome. We just trust God to keep us safe." Amazing how some things stick in our minds. Now there is a street named Dykes by the church. Rightfully so, I suppose.

As I was sitting there in the Tahoe in front of the house trying to decide whether or not to go to the door for information, a lady crossed the street in front of me. "Ma'am, may I ask you, do any of the Dykes family live in this house now?" "Yes, I do. I am the great- granddaughter of Wilmer and Hanna Dykes." "Really?" I exclaimed. "Let me explain why I am here." And I did. We chatted, and I learned about the present status of the church family. I thanked her and she went inside.

I pulled back in front of the church. I called home. Freda's voice was still on the answering service. I wanted to hear her voice. She answered in that soft sweet voice of hers. How strange—now forty-one years later, and life together has come and gone. And how quickly, it seems. Yet, she lives. I listened to her children singing on the CD. She lives in them and through them. As I pulled away, headed back to Tallahassee, she was singing "He's Been Faithful to Me": " . . . looking back, His love and mercy I see." Yes!

There was a quicker way back home, but I wanted to travel Highway 90 again. What a beautiful drive. And as I passed through Greenville, a little town the size of a flea, I remembered we were stopped there for speeding when traveling home to see family. The police took us to City Hall—a big deal in a little place. Her soft-spoken ways won the day. We left without a ticket. I was headed to the Community College in Lake City, where our relationship began. I pushed in the CD, "This Guy's in Love with You," which I first heard the day I realized I was in love with her. It started flooding; no, the water was in my eyes, not on my windshield.

It was getting dark. I wanted to make it to her gravesite before dark. And I did. I left the music playing as I walked to her resting place. "Have I told you lately that I love you, that there is no one above you? . . ." was playing.

My loss seemed like yesterday, not a year and a half ago. I sat and gripped the gravestone with my arms. I cried out, "I can't get over you. I keep saying to myself I look forward but your love keeps pulling me back to you. Without you, I feel so exposed to a world that knows little of your kind of love. Yes,

I know, I know. In time your love will push me forward. That's what real love does."

"Today, with you, sweetheart, was so wonderful. Thank you for your love for me—for family."

Well, a fitting pilgrimage for a Memorial Day. And now the future—"Oh God, the future. Help me sort it all out; help my spirit catch breath again."

This is where resolve comes in. Everything within me wants to hold on. But love doesn't live in the past; it lives in the present and the future. Love does push us forward toward life and contribution. Only resolve will allow us to overcome the pull of our emotions toward the past. In the end, I guess, love and resolve are one in the same. Or maybe better said, resolve is an expression of love. That's why, in the end, love will push us forward.

Now the projects . . .

PART THREE
THE PROJECTS OF HOPE
The Gifts of Love

CHAPTER FOURTEEN
Our Home

Projects. Freda and I always had projects going on. Hers. Mine. Ours. And usually multiples at one time. And I have had projects which coincide with my pilgrimage of grief that have helped me along the way.

First one, our home. Freda and I built three homes together across the years of our marriage, the last in 2006. She was doing okay again, health-wise, and we were provided an opportunity by the Lord for a piece of property with a hill overlooking a beautiful pastoral setting. We decided to build. Freda, for the most part, designed the home. And she did well—a home with lots of openness and spacious views, situated for sunrises and sunsets. She enjoyed our home for three years. The problem: her health deteriorated consistently over this period of time; therefore, she was unable to complete the move-in with boxes left unpacked in the garage and decoration unfinished. Although the home was beautiful, it was incomplete.

One of the things I set out to do was to finish the move-in and the home furnishings. My understanding of her interests and desires was my guide. With help, especially from our daughter Christa and a family friend skilled in décor, family photos were framed and mounted. The study took the theme of heritage: "Remember the men from whence you came" (a Scottish proverb reflecting my Scottish heritage), with pictures of our forefathers dating back to the Civil War. The children's room took on an outdoor theme with photographs, wood panels, and burlap curtains, one bath with a seaside theme, and the master bath with water scenes from Europe, the Western Amazon Basin in Brazil, and lakes special to us. The bedroom, light blue and white, has been described as a "room in Heaven." With all my other responsibilities, it took over a year to complete. But I enjoyed the adventure, learned a lot in the process, experienced many bittersweet moments, of course. But with the help of family and friends, it was done.

On November 12, 2010, the one-year anniversary of her home-going, we celebrated with family and friends in our home. The house was beautifully adorned, the evening was cool and clear, the friends were warm and affirming. Freda would have been so excited—not so much about her home—but about the people she loved and enjoyed. Somehow, I felt we had finished this work together. When I retired for rest late that night, I did so with a feeling of gratitude and satisfaction.

Perhaps the final piece of art that we placed in our home will help you understand.

Freda, as mentioned earlier, was close to her maternal grandparents. She was in their home after her birth. The home place was the setting for the original home—a two-story wood frame house built of pine and oak on a stone foundation with a tin roof and stone chimney—now nearly a century old. It still stands, not strong, yet with a stately grace. Many memories were made with family and friends from her childhood to her last Christmas season.

The idea was to take weathered wood from the house, find an artist who could paint the house on the original wood, and place the unique piece above the fireplace in our family room. I found the artist, Rick Chance.

After enjoying a conversation with one of Freda's aunts, now in her nineties, I asked and received permission to choose the wood from the house with the help of the artist and the home decorator, Ingrid Crawford, who had been so helpful. We chose a wood door panel, still in good condition.

The painting of the old home on the door, which still has the handle attached, was beyond my expectation. It's a mirror image of the old home, the colors are well chosen, and it radiates an ambience of warmth and memories. In my mind I could see the smile come across Freda's face as the special piece of art was placed above the mantle. Each time I look at it, I am reminded of the treasured place of family in her life. Now the story can cast its shadow over the generations to come.

Now, maybe it's better understood when I say, "I felt we had finished 'moving in' together," especially after the same artist had painted her portrait, showing her standing, gracefully, and with a big smile, at the front door of our home. The portrait now hangs in the dining room and is seen as you walk into our home. Yes, it now seems complete.

Completion, as you will learn, is an important part of the healing work of grief. Completion—as much as is possible, that is.

Then there was the book . . .

CHAPTER FIFTEEN
The Prayer Book

In May 1998, Freda began a prayer group for women, especially in support of our staff wives. She wrote letters to the women each month. She did this to the very end, except a few times when she was physically unable to do so, at which time Mary Alice Dennis provided the needed support. It was my desire to edit these letters and publish them, making them available to others. With the help of my assistant, Diane McAlhany, and Dr. Fran Terhune, who worked diligently with me on editing, this work was completed within the year as well. It was published under the title, *Until My Last Breath,* and was made available to our wonderful church family that loved her deeply and supported her endlessly.

While on a recent trip to Africa, Charlotte Cearley, wife of Tim Cearley, Strategy Leader, Sub-Saharan African Peoples, who had received a copy of the book and had read it, made this comment to me:

> At first I was concerned that the book might be hard to read, full of sadness and death. What I found instead was this vibrant life, constantly learning and growing, especially in the area of prayer. She rarely focused on her own situation, except to ask for prayer. I felt encouraged and challenged as I read how she truly LIVED "until [her] last breath."

Freda's letter of October 23, 2006 is very personal and picturesque.

WAIT FOR THE LORD
October 23, 2006

Wait for the Lord;
Be strong and take heart
and wait for the Lord.

Psalm 27:14

God blessed me with a very special memory and word from Him in one of my prayer times last week. I remembered a very cold December morning when I was five years old. My mother, brother, and I lived with my maternal grandparents. I heard my mother calling me, but I was slow in getting to the house. When I arrived, there was no one there. (I found out later that my mother and grandmother had to leave for an appointment and thought that I was with my grandfather.) I went into the house and walked a long hallway to a gas heater where I sat down in a big, soft chair. I wondered where everyone was, but just knew my grandfather would come in at any time. I dozed off and on and don't know how long I had waited when I heard the footsteps in the hallway. I looked up and there was my grandfather walking down the hall toward me. He smiled and reached down with his long arms. He picked me up, sat down, wrapped those arms around me, and we began to talk. It was such a precious, joyful time that I remember it to this day. I waited with absolute assurance that he would come and then enjoyed the special time we had together.

But as for me,
I watch in hope for the Lord,
I wait for God my Savior;
My God will hear me.
Micah 7:7

God wants us to sit quietly with full confidence in Him and wait for Him to come to us just as I waited as a five-year-old child for my grandfather to come to me. My worrying, working, or frantic activity would not have brought my grandfather or solved any problems. The same is true in our relationship with God. We need to trust with the confidence of a child, and we need to wait before Him and enjoy the conversation and the love and security that come in our time with Him. As a child, I "worshiped" my earthly grandfather, but he was not perfect and all knowing. However, that relation-ship enabled me to understand something of my relationship with a heavenly Father who loves me completely and perfectly. Yet, how often do I miss the peace and security He affords and the joy that comes in my time with Him. The memory last week caused me to stop, wait, and spend even more time with Him than usual. What a glorious time it was! You may not have a grandfather like I did, but you have a loving heavenly Father who wants to spend time with you. Don't miss the blessings that come with that time.

It is my hope that this resource of prayer and testimony of a life well lived, will be an encouragement to many in the years to come.

CHAPTER SIXTEEN
The Songs

Another desire the Lord placed on my heart was to do a CD of songs that reflected her life, our relationship, and my gratitude for her love. At this writing, two songs have been completed, both with the assistance of a gifted young musician by the name of Mike Ricks.

The first title, "Pilgrim," was birthed by the loneliness that grips me, especially when I arrive at home each night to be alone. We worked with musicians from Nashville and a vocalist from west Florida. It was an exciting adventure for me—and again, a learning experience. The prayer book and the *Pilgrim* CD were presented as a gift to friends on the evening of celebration in our home.

Here are the lyrics to "Pilgrim":

I set out on the road again,
trying to find where we begin.
Can't take the thought of going home,
'cuz there without you I'm alone.
So I stop and I stare at where we first met
the way you looked, I will never forget.
Your hair was blowing in the winds of change,
my life would never be the same.
Now I'm a pilgrim on this journey of pain,
searching for reasons to live again.
And I'll try to be the best that I can.
Baby, without you, I'm a different man.
And I stop and I stare at my wedding band,
I wish I could go back to hold your hand.
I need you near me like never before,
my heart is broken, lying on the floor.

I'm not gonna give up, I'm not gonna run,

so many reasons to carry on.

I've got my Jesus, I've got our kids,

and in their faces I see you again.

In their eyes I see you again.

It's in their smiles I see you again.

The second song, "Until My Last Breath," was written by Mike Ricks as well and was inspired by Freda's love and commitment to missions. It was distributed at our World Missions Conference in March 2011. As you may imagine, it was a moving moment for me and the church family.

Here are the lyrics to "Until My Last Breath":

Grew up in a simple town.

The kinda place they don't write about.

Pastor's in the pulpit,

Momma's in her pew.

Heard the call to go to a distant land,

told Him I would follow,

my life was His to use,

no matter what may lie ahead.

I will climb every mountain in view,

I'll cross every ocean blue,

for Jesus I will not rest,

until my last breath.

Two kids later and a million miles,

been all over, seen a million smiles.

We'd go out and tell them of the hope we had found,

showed them they could trust in Jesus now.

Sometimes they would ask me

why I traveled just to see

a million hungry faces in need.
I never knew just how far that I would go
until the doctors said there's nothing they could do.
So I got down on my knees
and begged my Savior please,
send me to another needing you.
I have climbed every mountain in view,
crossed every ocean blue,
carried by Jesus through every test,
I will give Him nothing less.
For my Jesus I will not rest,
until my last breath.

There are still songs to be written and produced. Clearly, this project will take some time. It is my hope that, when finished, the songs will inspire others, as well as reflect the love of Freda and for Freda.

CHAPTER SEVENTEEN
The Scholarship Fund

Speaking of missions—at her loss, a mission scholarship fund was set up in her honor. To date the support has influenced work in five countries. This is the testimony of Christina Sweeney, one scholarship recipient:

I received the Freda Crawford Scholarship for my trip to the Amazon River Basin in Brazil. I was very thankful because it helped send me on the mission trip to serve the people in the small village of San George, and to show me the path God had for my life. The goal of our trip was to show the shining light of our almighty Lord into the darkness of the Amazon through the building of personal relationships with the people there. Through the power and grace of our Savior, thirty-three individuals came to Christ out of a village of eighty people, and countless miracles occurred during our trip. The everyday activities at the village went well; the villagers were open to learning English, Vacation Bible School, and Bible studies. God blessed us with the weather also. It only rained when we were on the boat for meals or at night when we were sleeping. It was such a blessing to have things work out so smoothly. Another blessing we saw was a baptism of Jose, who dedicated his life to the Lord and wants to become the pastor of the village. The very second after his salvation, he wanted to be discipled, so that he could teach and witness to the others in the village.

The trip gave us a great opportunity to build relationships with the villagers and to fulfill their needs. The trip also helped me to strengthen my relationship with the Lord. It reconfirmed my heart for international missions and my heart for the

Amazon River Basin. At the time I was struggling with a call to vocational missions, but since this trip I have accepted my call as a missions minister. It is through the Freda Crawford Scholarship that I was able to go on this mission trip to Brazil and that I started to discover my call to vocational ministry. I am so grateful for the scholarship and for everything that Freda Crawford did for missions.

Christina is one of 150 at Westside who have received a call to vocational ministry or missions, now serving in ten states and nine countries. The heartbeat of Freda for missions was a strong influence in creating an environment in which God's call could be heard.

It's interesting that, as I write this, I am leaving South Africa after having met with the acting president of a theological school in Kenya, as well as the person who oversees missions work in forty-nine countries and 600 plus personnel. I was exploring the possibility of teaching at the school and engaging unengaged, unreached people groups. Though Freda was unable to travel with me to these two countries, her heart would have taken her there and her influence is felt through her book *Until My Last Breath* and her music. Seeing her passion and influence continue somehow helps me move toward closure.

While Freda had a heart for the world, she loved home, and the kitchen was a place she shared her love. Here is how she did that . . .

CHAPTER EIGHTEEN

The Cookbook

"Expression of Love – "Cooking in the Crawford Home"

Freda liked to cook. Cooking was a heritage from her grandmother BeBe and her mother, who thought of time in the kitchen as an investment in family. I share wonderful memories from around their table as well.

It was also, for Freda, an act of love. She would fragrance our entire home from the kitchen with the aroma of a nutritious meal or a special dessert loved by the family.

And mealtime was not just about enjoyable food with good nutrition. It was a time to pray, talk, read, and laugh. In short, it was a time to love. The meal was an expression of love for the most important people in her life—her family and friends.

Those who were little known and had little, as well as those who were world known and had much, sat at her table. And while the food was enjoyed, the sentiment of those who sat at the table was the warm hospitality, her interest in those present, and her ease of conversation were what made the meal "home-cooked" and what was most appreciated.

I am fortunate among men for such an expression of love to our family, friends, guests, and me.

The recipes in the book are selective—not comprehensive. For example, one of the special treats for family was the ever-popular Congo Bars:

2/3 cup liquid shortening
1 pound box brown sugar
3 eggs
2 and 2/3 cup self-rising flour*
1 cup pecans
1 (6oz) package chocolate chips
Bake at 350 degrees for 40 minutes in a greased oblong pan.

*For self-rising flour, add 1 1/2 teaspoons baking powder and 1/2 teaspoon salt to every cup of regular flour.

These come with memories and with the hope that they can help you make sweet memories with your family and friends as well.

I have already experienced benefit from the book. For example, our daughter Christa asked, "Can we keep a copy in your kitchen?" The answer was, "Of course." Our daughter-in-law Tina, as well as Christa, have used recipes in preparing food for our family—always a wonderful reminder of Freda and family.

Friends have also prepared certain foods from the recipes and shared them with me. Equally important, family and friends have challenged me to learn to cook and prepare such meals myself. That's happening . . . very slowly!

CHAPTER NINETEEN
God's Sustaining Hand—a Musical CD

After Freda's first bone marrow transplant, which failed and things were not looking good, I asked her to tape a couple of songs for the family. She did. Meantime, she had a second transplant, which was successful. After recovery, the two songs turned into a project—a CD involving the family and a few friends. The engineer was Greg Dole with Justice Road Studios, and the producer was Network Sound and Video. The primary motivation for the CD, other than for family, was to say thank you to the Westside family for their love and support. It included songs such as, "More Than Wonderful," a duet by Freda and Doug White; "Amazing Grace," featuring family; "Touch Through Me," her signature song; and others. On the front cover she wrote:

> *Dear Listeners,*
>
> *My prayer for you is that you have a personal relationship with Jesus Christ, and that your relationship with Him will grow each day. I also pray that you can hear my love for Him in this music. He has given me life and been so good to me. I will continue to praise Him as long as He gives me breath. After that, I will have the joy of praising Him face to face.*
>
> *"Because you are my help, I sing in the shadow of your wings. My soul clings to you; your right hand upholds me"* (Psalm 63:7-8).

And, as I wrote on the back cover:
> *William Blake was right in his poignant statement, "Life is joy and woe woven fine . . ." Yes, and God's grace is found in both and makes the joy richer and the woe serve His purpose. The selections of songs provide a few glimpses of her journey*

*of faith. It was her desire that the music would
encourage others to see "God's Sustaining Hand"
in life and family.*

After Freda's death, I did a redesign and re-produced it. The music has now found its way to other countries, as well as being heard here at home. Her music has been a great encouragement to me while on this pilgrimage. Our grandchildren, on their own, have memorized every song. I will always be grateful to the family for making this music a reality—and especially grateful to her.

Her signature song on the CD is "Touch through Me":

TOUCH THROUGH ME
by Barbara Tubbs

*Touch through me, Holy Spirit, touch through me,
Let my hands reach out to others, touch through me;
There's a lonely soul somewhere
needing just one friend to care,
Touch through me, Holy Spirit, touch through me.*

*Love through me, Holy Spirit, love through me,
I will be my brother's keeper, love through me;
Hearts are bleeding deep inside,
love can dry the weeping eye,
Love through me, Holy Spirit, love through me.*

*Flow through me, Holy Spirit, flow through me,
Like a river in the desert, flow through me;
Springing power and healing strength,
living water pure and clean,
Flow through me, Holy Spirit, flow through me.*

*My hands will be your hands reaching out to others,
My lips will not be slothful, Lord, to speak;
I will be that good Samaritan to someone else in need,
I will be your house to dwell in, live through me.*

*Flow through me, Holy Spirit, flow through me,
Holy Spirit, touch through me,
Holy Spirit, touch through me.*

These words expressed the desire of her heart and the commitment of her life. Of course, allowing the love of Christ to flow through us is God's intention for us all.

And it is our privilege.

CHAPTER TWENTY
The Memorial Prayer Garden

Freda was known for her prayer life and prayer leadership. Her book of edited prayer letters reflects this conviction and commitment of her life.

Included in our vision for the relocation of our church was a Prayer Garden. The church family initiated this work, not only in her honor, but as a statement of our "Prayer First" commitment.

Here is the statement to the church family:

> *The church family voted during the business meeting of July 21, 2010, to approve the construction of a very meaningful improvement on the grounds of the Westside Baptist Church, a memorial prayer garden dedicated to the memory of Freda Craw-ford. Freda Crawford, our pastor's wife, positively affected the lives of many individuals, the church family as a whole, the community of Gainesville, and remote parts of the world. She served along-side our pastor at Westside for over twenty-eight years. Her influence on the importance of prayer and missions has and continues to be the role model and basis for these on-going ministries at Westside Baptist Church. Therefore, it is only fit-ting to construct a prayer garden with a focus on the world and Westside Baptist Church's mission goal, "To bring the hope of Christ to all people," in memory of Freda Crawford.*

With the help of a lead team, including a design architect, an engineer, a landscape artist, the garden was completed and now stands as a constant reminder of the essential role of prayer in our lives and family. The garden includes a brick panorama of the world with our mission statement, "Bringing the hope of Christ to all people." The garden was awarded a city beautification award.

At the dedication, these words were spoken by a friend, Mike Nichols:

> *From the day of relocating to this property . . . the prayer garden we are dedicating today was a dream. Today that dream becomes a reality. Prayer has always been the lifeblood of Westside Baptist Church. You have prayed for your families, your community, your world . . . consistently and without apology. I am sure there are some standing before me today who were prayed over by Westside members before you came to Christ. This church knows the power of prayer.*
>
> *So as we dedicate this garden . . . it should be looked at as a visible launching pad for every ministry at Westside Baptist Church. Passersby will see it, you will use it, and God will be glorified by what happens on this plot of land.*
>
> *We are dedicating this property today in the memory of Freda Crawford. She embodied prayer and had a deep relationship with our Lord. From her prayer letters, that are now in print, to her leading prayer events for the women of Westside, and praying over and with people who walked through the halls of Westside, there could be no better representation of what this garden will stand for than Freda Crawford.*
>
> *It is interesting to me that I never had the opportunity to know Freda when she wasn't sick. But the woman that I knew was full of grace and energy. She was full of purpose. You don't live the way she lived and touch the lives she touched without a special relationship with the Father.*
>
> *As close as Freda and Gary were, I am not sure that even Gary knew the depth of sacrifice that it took for her to keep going. But the grace she*

needed for every day was there, and I personally believe, as the days got harder, her relationship grew deeper.

As I would stay at the home of Freda and Gary, I was given a firsthand look at the depth of Freda's life. If there could be a definition that describes the perfect pastor's wife, Freda embodied that definition.

I remember the earned doctorate with all the study and pain and prayer.

I remember her being just as driven for the cause of Christ, here and abroad, as Pastor Gary was. When the doctors said "You can't go" . . . she prayed.

I even remember her helping Gary on one of his sermons, even from the hospital.

I can remember her heading off to Nicaragua because of her deep love for her daughter and grandchildren. I bet she prayed a lot for all her grandchildren.

I came into town once and she had been working incessantly to help finish their book on marriage (like staying up all night). After working all night, and still very sick, Freda was speed walking. She just never stopped.

As she served alongside her husband in this ministry, she loved every minute of it. She taught, sang, prayed, and lives were touched through her. Westside was blessed by this prayer warrior.

God, in His grace, extended her journey long enough to be blessed by her grandchildren. I wonder how much prayer time she gave them. A lot.

Freda Crawford's life was built on prayer. I believe her journey here was lengthened by prayer. Eternity will only tell what was accomplished by her prayer life.

> *And now, we are dedicating in her name, a place of prayer. What greater legacy could anyone achieve than having a place of prayer be forever established in his or her honor. Today we are all privileged to dedicate this prayer garden to such to a woman of prayer, Freda Crawford.*
>
> *"Then I heard a voice from heaven say, 'Write: Blessed are the dead who die in the Lord from now on. Yes,' says the Spirit, 'they will rest now from their labor for their deeds will follow them'"* (Revelation 14:13).

Soon after its completion, we held our World Missions Conference and nineteen missionaries, representing eleven countries stood in the garden and prayed hand-in-hand—a fitting picture of Freda's life commitment. Since then, it is a real joy for me to see folks there reflecting and praying. And I must say, every time I drive up to our church and see the fountain bubbling water like a brook, it is an oasis to me, a symbol of her presence and continuing influence, a reminder of her love, and a strength for me to carry on.

My family and I are so grateful for the love and good will of our church family and their commitment to prayer.

CHAPTER TWENTY-ONE
The Biography

One other project is in my sights: a biography of Freda's life. Why? Because I carry the conviction that it will encourage and inspire all who read it. Perhaps in due time it will be done. Here is the introduction to the book:

Why does this book exist?

Freda Crawford was certainly beloved by a lot of people, especially me, but hers is not a household name. Yes, she had an impact on her world. On me, as her husband. On our children. On our grandchildren. Our extended family. Our church family at Westside Baptist Church in Gainesville, Florida. On her colleagues and students at Buccholz High School and the University of Florida. On the doctors and medical staff who treated her during what became a ten-year battle against multiple myeloma.

She was an encourager.

She had a brilliant mind, a servant's heart, an angelic voice, and beautiful feet.

She had incredible reserves of strength and fortitude that still amaze to this day.

She was my best friend, and I miss her.

But why should *you* get to know her?

What was so special about Freda Crawford that would merit an entire book on her life? She was certainly no saint. Her name won't find its way into textbooks, and we won't find her face on a postage stamp any time soon. She was just an ordinary human being who struggled with the same doubts, concerns, and physical limitations as the rest of us.

And yet . . .

Talk to the people who knew her and watch them light up. I know it's easy for me to say—I was her husband, so I'm biased. But it really is true. When people talk about her to those who never had any contact with her, they inevitably say, "I wish you'd known her."

Freda was an extraordinarily ordinary person who changed the world by changing the world around her.

In other words, she was just like you.

Freda Crawford was a lifelong learner, which made her a natural teacher, and she took those talents into every aspect of her life. She was always intentionally looking to learn from every situation, from every possible perspective, and point of view. And because she was so intent on learning, she was also intent on teaching.

Yes, Freda was a teacher, both literally through her work at Buccholz High School, the University of Florida, and as a Bible study teacher at Westside Baptist Church, but she was also subtly, and perhaps even unknowingly, teaching those around her. Teaching about life. About parenting. About relational dynamics in life.

About her faith. About her love for Jesus.

About prayer.

Freda was most definitely a woman of prayer. She saturated her day in prayer and, some say, lived her life as a prayer.

In Luke 11, the disciples ask Jesus an important question, the answer to which is the Lord's Prayer, the most famous—and most recited—prayer of all time. The question is this: "Lord, teach us to pray."

Teach. Pray.

We all must pray. We all must be taught.

We are, all of us, learners.

We are, all of us, teachers.

I wrote this book, not as a way of lionizing my wife—she would have hated that. The very fact that this book exists would've galled her to no end. If I'd told her I was going to write a book about her life, she would have told me to write about something more interesting and more important.

But that's just the thing. Because my hope is, in learning about Freda, you will learn something more interesting and more important: you will learn about yourself, you will learn about Jesus and His love for you, and you will learn about life—a well-lived life.

He really does love you. Honestly.

This book isn't *really* about Freda. It's about all of us. It's about the human condition and the choices we have to make as we live our lives, the daily, rubber-meets-the-road decisions that govern us.

Freda had to make those choices, and they may astound you.

My prayer is that you will read this story and find yourself in these pages. And as you do, you will learn more about a Savior who so desperately loves you that He gave it all up for you.

And now, let me introduce you to an extraordinarily ordinary woman. My wife, Freda.

Amen.

The question has been asked, "Why do such projects as these—they just keep you focused on the past." Well, I beg to differ. While rooted in the past, they are acts of love in the present. They are means of involving family and friends and building on her legacy and nurturing her continued influence. To me, they have been a healing balm. And it is my prayer that these acts of love will encourage others for years to come—including you.

Now, a look at the things that matter—ultimately . . .

PART FOUR
THE GIFT OF LOVE
What Ultimately Matters

CHAPTER TWENTY-TWO
Family

Freda was loved and respected by family. This is because of her deep love for her family and her common sense approach to life. Members of the family, old and young, often sought her practical wisdom and personal perspective. She was a family matriarch, ask any member of the family. Hear the words from our son John:

One on each knee

Daddy held her, Daddy held me.

Smile on his face, love in his heart

Mamma took the picture, she always did her part.

More pretty than Dad was handsome, full of grace and then some

I wish I knew her more.

Daddy's smile made up for Granddaddy being gone

Mamma was there when Daddy wasn't.

She made life real and our house a home.

I wish I knew what life was like in her mind.

Daddy must have loved her well.

She gave herself and then some more.

She was a mom and a southern belle.

I wish I grew up with both of them.

I wonder what she thought about.

She was a girl and then a woman.

Did she like home, did she ever want out?

I wish she would have told me.

I never asked what I wanted to know.

I never asked what I didn't.

Time moves fast and understanding is slow.

I wish I could have understood more.

Pictures don't tell the truth.

Vain attempts to freeze time.

They don't give what we know and never knew.

I wish I knew what life was like before I was here.

One on each side

Me and my sister still here with him.

Carrying on with her inside

We did not think much then about the end.

More endings are to come.

Dad is here and his smile keeps on.

Where is Granddaddy or Mamma's Dad?

I missed them when they were here.

I wish we understood.

I remember Dad's knee.

I remember my smile.

From there to here seems like only a little while.

Mamma's touch is gone for good.

I would turn back time only if I could.

I can't.

My sister is grown up.

Daddy is older now.

Mamma is gone.

Maybe my only hope is my own.

Maybe I can sit one on each knee.

If I can have Daddy's smile,

If I can have that time, what will we be?

Father help me to know.

Keep time full. Keep it slow.

When he grows up, what will he write?

Help his center be on you.
We can't freeze time even though we try.
Why does it hurt that we can't go back?
I wish I grew up with them.
Take me into those pictures.
Take me home.
I wish I knew them more.
All of them.

And catch the words of her nine-year-old grandson Michael, shared with the family and then at the dedication of the Memorial Prayer Garden:

When Digi is at home
I am never alone

When Digi is at home
I will never roam

When I think about her
Being gone, my heart groans

When I think about her being gone
I want to call her on the phone

When I think of her being STRONG
Then I have grown

Freda wasn't a perfect mom or grandmother but one thing was clear—she loved deeply and family came first. When the force of her love and presence was gone, the vacuum was felt by all.

When I lost Freda, the family came to my side immediately. In the midst of pressing responsibilities of their own, they cried with me, walked with me, stood with me, made decisions with me, and in time laughed with me. In the midst of the challenges of owning their own business, both my son John and son-in-law Bill were present as much as possible during those first few months and available by the ring of the phone.

My daughter Christa, "Princess" to me, knew the reality of stabbing pain at the loss of her mother. I remember when John and I returned home from Little Rock, her gripping hug. I shall never forget the look in her tear-filled eyes—a look of compassion for me in my broken state, and at the same time I saw the grief-laden question that begged an answer: "What now, Dad?" Later that evening, as we lay on the bed in Freda's and my bedroom, she grabbed her mom's pillow, wrapping her arms around it, muffling her cries for her mother. Maybe it was there, on that pillow, in that moment, that she found the strength she would need—for she has been strong. I see so much of her mother in her—her beautiful eyes, the graceful way she carries herself, and the values she holds. I'm so proud of her.

Sitting by the bed were John, Bill, and Tina—my daughter-in-law, whom I call "Angel." She and Freda had spent much time together over the previous three years in large measure due to the enjoyment they received in their relationship and because of Lachlan, our new grandson. Freda knew her time with her precious grandchildren, then Cade, Michael, Johanna, and Lachlan, might be cut short. She wanted every moment possible with them, no matter the cost to her own well-being.

Tina, too, felt the loss deeply. This memory is vivid. A few weeks had passed. It was Christmas time. That evening, we were at the Christmas Festival our church provides for the city of Gainesville. Thousands of people attend. Freda and I, along with our grandchildren, would ride in the sleigh during the performance. This year, Freda was absent. It was on this particular evening, just Lachlan and me were to ride in the sleigh, when Tina came to my office with Lachlan. She was overwhelmed by the sadness of the moment—Christmas without Mom. She wept uncontrollably. What special times they had enjoyed—now, sweet memories at best.

Tina was Freda's friend. I will forever be grateful for the joy Tina brought into her life. And I, too, have enjoyed and benefited from friendship with Tina. I'm so proud of her as well.

Christa has sorely missed her mom and the pilgrimage has

been difficult—and still is. And Tina traveled her own path
of healing. But, as they grieved, they walked with me in my
own pilgrimage. They did so in many tangible ways. You may
say I was a "kept man" by Freda. The way she cared for me
spoiled me. Needless to say, I was lost without her. The girls,
Christa and Tina, were there for me as I learned to live life
without Freda.

Their shoulders were always there for me at those unexpected moments of pain. They have taught me much about
cooking, nutrition, and caring for a home, and helped to make
the children available to me when I may most enjoy them or
find solace in them. We worked in the garden together, learned
to can vegetables, put up vegetables for the freezer as Freda did
so consistently over the years. She always had a freezer full of
fresh foods.

In addition, they both encouraged and shared times of exer-
cise, arranged special times for fun, and always kept a watchful
eye on me. They have been healers for my soul. I'm grateful for
them both—and for all my family.

A chronic illness within the family is tough on all of the
family. It affects family life in conscious and unconscious ways.
It is best for a family to know this and address this together. And
then, when the loss comes, an adjustment has to be made. But
this can be confusing and challenging. This is what I learned
about family in the process of grieving our loss that may be
helpful to you.

First, the memorial service is a critically important part of
the process. It's so significant because it connects us with our
faith, family, and friends. It is a time of remembrance, reflection,
tribute, celebration, and most importantly, a time of worship.

For my family and me, the time of preparation for the service was invaluable. As we sat around the dining room table,
sipping coffee, and sorting through hundreds of photographs,
reflecting on experiences of the past, laughing and crying, it
gave us an opportunity to relive the best of times and celebrate
our most wonderful memories, while at the same time, creating

an important memory of what it means to be family.

Margaret Dickens, a friend of Freda and the family, and our chosen director, provided excellent guidance for the service, which was delayed for several days to allow friends from around the country to attend. The service was filled with faith, hope, tribute, and celebration. It was an important marker toward healing and a witness of a life well lived. I would encourage any family to maximize the opportunity that a memorial service offers.

Second, understand that each member of the family grieves according to personality, the particular relationship, and ability to connect with one's own feelings or willingness to do so. It is a mistake to place our own expectations on others—and unfair. To accept one another for who they are and where they are is to love well. That is what each member of the family most needs.

Third, the loss of a spouse is unique—especially in a long marriage and a close-knit family life. To expect children who have lost their mother to understand what it's like to lose one's life mate is another mistake that can be made. With Freda's homegoing, I lost the *"wife of my youth"* (see Malachi 2:14) and the love of my life. She was the mother of my children, my cohort in ministry, my comrade in arms for the challenges in life, my counselor, and my friend. I cannot expect my loss to be the same loss that others experience. For our children, who loved their mother deeply, the loss was heavy—just different. And so it was with each member of the family, and with friends. I discovered the best way we can help each other is to be accepting and helpful in ways that are truly meaningful to each person in his or her own particular experience of grief.

Fourth, communication is imperative. One may be more verbal than another, and one may desire to talk more frequently than another or more deeply than another. Each of these can vary on any given day. The important thing is to provide an environment of safety and to talk, and keep talking. These conversations are windows into one another's soul. When we see what is there, we can embrace it and in embracing it, we move together through grief. Given the busyness of our lives, this will require, for most of us, a real commitment to create time for this dialogue to happen. Given the context of our lives, this was a special challenge for my family and me. How well we did, I think, will be revealed over time. One thing is certain—there is a window when such conversation is most important. Capture it.

Questions. Asking no questions or the wrong questions will ensure progressive distance and possibly failure in family. Asking the right questions, in the right way, and right time will ensure that a family will experience progressive growth and success. Of all the questions that might be asked, I believe these three questions offer the best possibilities for a growing understanding and love: "What do I do that disappoints you?" "What can I do better or differently?" "What is your inside story?" When these questions are asked sincerely and the answers understood and responded to with respect and change, good things happen. And these questions can be especially helpful in a time of grief when the family needs one another the most.

Fifth, planning experiences together that are meaningful, fun, and nurturing demonstrates that family remains first. There is no greater protection for the family and no greater gift. We planned and enjoyed time in the mountains, at the beach, in our homes, and with extended family. Yes, there was a sense that something was missing—and there was—a *someone*. But there was also a sense of legacy that brought good memories, joy, and hope into the present and future.

Sixth, tradition. The Christmas following the homegoing of Freda was difficult. Yet, on Christmas Eve, we attended the worship service at Westside with all its warmth and celebration. Then, as we gathered in our home filled with the aroma of chili, the fireplace flickering, the tree with its bright lights, the gifts which had been selected with love, the Bible to give interpretation and meaning to it all, there was a sense of her presence—a sense of rightness about this tradition that has brought its special joy to us across the years. We are finding that honoring established traditions and seeking to build new ones are ways not only to honor the loved one, but also to bring healing and to look toward the future. Traditions bring the past into the present and move the present into the future. Traditions—some stay, some change, but their practice gives continuity to life.

Seventh, pay special attention to the children. Children suffer from grief in a similar way as we do as adults, but with even less understanding. My experience leads me to say that children know more than what we give them credit for. We want to protect them and often harm them by our good intentions. We rob them of honesty, of inclusion, and of developing coping skills. According to some, preschoolers generally view death as temporary. Children, ages five to nine, view death as permanent, but may personify death as a ghost. Children age ten through teenage years may resist talking about their feelings. Being young, they may think of death as distant and not consider it on a personal level. Nonetheless, all children respond to death with some level of grief. How we respond to them is important.

Here some things that I have learned over the years about relating to children. I hope that you may find these thoughts helpful:

- Acknowledge their grief.
- Be open and responsive to their questions.
- Include them in the family gathering, the viewing, the funeral, and other appropriate times. However, be careful not to make a child do what clearly he or she is not ready to do.
- Choose your language carefully. The person didn't really "pass away," a phrase that may have multiple meanings for a child. The person died. The same is true for "journey." The child may fear you going on a journey and not coming back. Even if the Biblical term "sleep" is used, explain it. Otherwise, the child may be afraid to go to bed. It is best not to say a person is "with Jesus" unless that is explained. Otherwise, children may be angry at Jesus for taking their loved one.

- Expect the child to have questions and simple observations in the months to come. Things are on their mind, even when we think not. For example, on one occasion, our daughter-in-law was on the phone with a friend. While in conversation, her cell phone rang. Lachlan, then three years old, picked it up and starting talking as if he was in conversation with someone. After his mom got off the phone, she asked him, "Who were you talking to?" He replied, "Digi (Freda)." "And what did she say?" "She said you are to give me some cookies!" The point—she was on his mind. On another occasion he was with me at home. We were watching "David and Goliath" on DVD. He seemed very focused on the movie. Suddenly, he turned to me and said, "Digi loved me." She was on his mind.

I came home from being gone for a week. On the counter was a note from Johanna, our seven-year-old granddaughter:
I love you. I also miss Digi. I think of the things that she did with me. I like when we spend the night. I know Gpa feels sad in his heart about Digi. I love Digi and Gpa. One day we will see Digi again.

Our children are very much aware of loss. They think. They feel. They question. It is best if we are conscious of this and be present for them. And, don't forget, we can learn from them as well.
- When we don't have answers, be honest. If answers can be sought together, the question becomes a teachable moment.
- Share good memories and funny experiences. This brings comfort to the child—to all of us.
- Love them well. Provide extra affection. Remember, they are dealing with loss as well.

Children are precious. They are gifts from the Lord. Our experiences mold and shape us. If we are attentive, understanding, truthful, and loving, we can help them toward maturity.

Eighth, celebrate. Look for opportunities to celebrate the best in life. This creates a positive focus and helps us simply enjoy the presence of one another. Celebrating the little things can be as meaningful as one big thing. The notes and photographs on the refrigerator door, the principles for a "healthy, happy day" that served us for thirty-five years framed and hung on the wall, and even how we say "bye." When we are leaving one of our homes, the family leaving rolls down the windows of their vehicle, the remaining family members stand in the drive. Then, as the others drive away, all wave and yell, "Bye! Bye! Bye!" It's kind of a way of saying, "I don't really want to leave, but I will see you soon." A way of saying, I guess, "You're special."

I remember, growing up, that my maternal grandparents always had a way of making you feel special when arriving or leaving their home. When arriving, no matter what they were doing, they would stop and give attention to you. They would stand, greet you with a warm handshake or hug, and focus on your interests. When leaving, they would walk you to the door, open it for you, walk to the porch or driveway, stand and say, "Bye," and see you out of sight. Yes, I know things have changed—still the principle of helping others feel welcome and special is what Christ does for us and what we are to do for each other. This is especially important during these times of change and uncertainty.

Finally. Doing your estate planning before crisis comes is an act of love. It can't change everything that comes with the loss of a loved one, but it can make things easier or more difficult. Planning can work to protect your family or create pain. Giving attention to having a will, appropriate insurance, and other matters of estate is simply wise and right.

Yes, family runs deep. Let me explain with this journal entry:
*The morning was bright, cool, and beautiful—
the kind of spring day you want to be eternal. My
Tahoe hummed toward Lake City—it was family
that beckoned the priority: the Easter 2010 meal*

gathering for extended family.

I arrived. Hearty welcome was given to every-one by everyone. The crowd seemed a bit smaller. It seems to diminish a bit each year. While it is true that those present are the very young to the very old, the older generations are best represented. Why? A number of reasons, I suppose. One is value. It seems to be valued most by the older. And why is that? Perhaps such a gathering was a family value in the culture of their day that has remained so. Maybe because they have a vantage point in life that the end can be seen more clearly than the beginning, and family relationships become more sacred, more cherished, as we realize the fleeting of time. Maybe it's the progressive realization of our own mortality.

As I talked with one, then another, I marveled at the new life of infants, now seven generations from our patriarch and matriarch. Talking with others, one has had back surgery and another pending back surgery, another dealing unsuccessfully with cancer, and some will never be with us again, including my own Freda. Still the memories were shared, the jokes told, the adages of the family sages are quoted, and hope renewed. Somehow the extended view of the family past makes the present more enjoyable, more important, and the future look more hopeful. No wonder the Scripture says, "God sets the lonely in families" (Psalm 68:6). We are all lonely without family. As I leave, I do so with a bit more resolve toward nurturing such a heritage—even in the midst of the now cultural challenges toward family—no—especially because of present cultural challenges.

Knowing our heritage strengthens our own sense of identity.

We can't fully know who we are unless we know who they were. In them we find our own strengths and weaknesses, our own honor, or maybe failure. We learn about hopes and dreams, about possibilities, about relationships. We are reminded that we are not only the nuclear family; we are community. Our heritage—our legacy—and our traditions give us insight and strength beyond our own. This is the only antidote for our families awash in the cultural sea of brokenness and loneliness with no sense of the past, no glue for the present, and no hope for the future.

And one other thing. Respect for the older generation. Not only respect but humility to learn, the wisdom to find counsel, the willingness to listen and understand heritage.

While on a recent trip to Kenya, in a conversation with Dr. Linus Kirimi, I learned about the Mzee (pronounced Unzee), the word for an old and respected man. He explained that, in his culture, age is valued for the experience and wisdom it brings. There is a council of older men who grapple with the needs and issues of families and community and offer guidance. He spoke of the stability that tradition brings as one generation transitions into another. As Scripture says, " . . . *children are a crown to the aged, and parents are the pride of their children*" (Proverbs 17.6).

The Bible has much to say about respect for elders, and about godly heritage as a basis for living in the present and planning for the future. We would be wise to heed God's counsel and to make the effort to be a part of the larger community of family.

I leave the reunion and visit the cemetery where Freda's body lies beneath the beauty of the flowers. The marker quotes Song of Songs, *"How delightful is your love, my friend, my bride"* (4:10). It was and it is. As the song says, " . . . my love will follow you, stay with you, you are never alone."

As I stood there at her foot, I talk to her as if she were looking at me intently with those big, brown, beautiful eyes—waiting to respond. "I'm so grateful the Lord placed you in my life. It's tough without you. I keep trying to love our children and grandchildren well, to help keep our family focused on family, to keep the church family you loved under the best care I have to offer, and to learn how to live without you by my side. Though alone, after four decades with you, I'm much better prepared for the years to come. That's because your love, courage, strength, and adventurous spirit lives on within me. As your marker states of you, "A life well lived"—I pray that will be true of mine.

As I left, I walked past the graves of my parents, grand-parents, her grandparents, and the beloved Pastor Henry Cumbie and his wife. (He once said from the pulpit as we sat together in that little country church as teenagers—"Your smiles will be a bright spot in the Kingdom work in the years to come.") There in the cemetery, I was reminded of a simple, but poignant scriptural truth:

"As a father has compassion on his children, so the Lord has compassion on those who fear him; for He knows how we are formed, he remembers that we are dust. As for man, his days are like grass, he flourishes like a flower in the field; the wind blows over it and it is gone, and its place remembers it no more. But from everlasting to everlasting the Lord's love is with those who fear him, and his righteousness with their children's children." (Psalm 103:13-17)

No wonder the Bible says, *"Teach us to number our days aright, that we may gain a heart of wisdom"* (Psalm 90:12) and *"Satisfy us in the morning with your unfailing love, that we may sing for joy and be glad all our days"* (Psalm 90:14).

Family, to me, is life. Nurture family, love well, and when their presence, love, and support are most needed, it will be given. That is my experience and for that I'm grateful beyond measure. Yes, I know, many are on hard times in family. That is both sad and regrettable, and we as a family have our own challenges. But the principle stands—a loving family is, outside of God himself, the greatest healer of hurt. We often prepare when guests are coming. We clean house, we tidy up, we put our best foot forward. And that is understood. However, I believe it is important to treat family as guests in the sense of priority, courtesy, and best foot forward. I know family is the place to be ourselves, to let our hair down, for life in its most raw form—at its best and worst. That's family. I'm just vying for the principle of treating family for who they are, that is, the most important people in our lives, with the same courtesy and positive behavior as guests. This makes for a strong family. And remember, the church family can be like family. This is especially important when our own families are on hard times. The Church is God's healing family of faith.

CHAPTER TWENTY-THREE
Friends

Some People
Some people come into our lives and quickly go.
Some people move our souls to dance.
They awaken us to new understanding with the passing whisper of their wisdom.
Some people make the sky more beautiful to gaze upon.
They stay in our lives for a while,
Leave footprints on our hearts,
And we are never, ever the same.

True friendship is a rare jewel. We all want good friends, need good friends; yet deep and lasting friendships are not a given. When experienced, they are to be treasured, protected, and nurtured.

Friends have played such an important role for Freda and me; especially during the decade she fought her battle. And now, especially, for me since her loss. They have been traveling partners on our pilgrimage. We feel we owe a debt to each.

One of my favorite statements defining a friend is "Someone who steps in when all others have stepped out." And one of my favorite examples of friendship is that between David and Jonathan. It is said that *". . . the soul of Jonathan was knit to the soul of David, and Jonathan loved him as his own soul"* (1 Samuel 18:1, KJV). Wow! What a special relationship.

As I reviewed the story of their relationship, I saw the essentials of such a close relationship. It was based on a covenant of love (see 1 Samuel 18:3). That is, it was rooted in the only thing that makes for a lasting and fulfilling relationship—love. That love was expressed through giving (18:4) which is the nature of love. They protected one another (19:2-3), always on the lookout for the best interest of the other. They didn't talk of friendship—they walked as friends, demonstrating their willingness to do whatever necessary to meet the needs of the other. *"Whatever you want me to do, I'll do for you"* (20:4), said Jonathan to David. Not only that, they expressed their love. *"They kissed each other and wept together"* (20:41). How unusual for men, especially in their context and culture, and for us, in our sexualized culture. And encouragement was woven into the fabric of their relationship: *"Jonathan . . . encouraged him in God"* (23:16).

This is the kind of friendship that we all want and need. Once when staying with friends, I left a note on the lamp table beside the bed which said, "I feel better about myself when I'm with you." This is one of the great benefits of a good friendship, increasing our self-worth—moving us toward our best selves. Of course, this is not to say that a good friend won't confront us with our less than best attitude or behavior. He or she will, as part of being a good friend—*"the pleasantness of one's friend springs from his earnest counsel"* and *"wounds from a friend can be trusted"* (Proverbs 27:9, 6). I am convinced this positive reinforcement should occur within family as well as outside of family with our other friends. In fact, family friendships make the best family and the best friends. But such friendships can be hard to come by for many reasons: a culture that has turned friendship into a commodity, our own fear of risk, of rejection, even the fear of love. As a result we wear masks. As Paul Tournier states, "We conceal our person behind a protective mask." It's a strange quirk of our nature to sabotage what we most need, but we do.

Tournier was incisively right when he observed, "No one can develop freely in the world and find a full life without feeling understood by at least one person." We would agree, wouldn't we? No wonder God said, *"It's not good for man to be alone"* (Genesis 2:18).

Johnny White and I met thirty-five years ago. We met at the childcare center at Southwestern Seminary. For a couple of years we shared classes and ministry. Now for the last thirty years, we have been separated by direction in ministry, 1,000 miles, and infrequent conversation. But each time we do talk, no matter how long it has been, it's like we pick up where we left off. In one of our last conversations by phone, I raised the question, "Johnny, what has kept our friendship over time and distance?" In his reply, one sentence imprinted on my mind. He said, "We have chosen to be there." He's right. In the end, our best friendships, our longest lasting friendships, are those in which we "choose" to be there as an act of love. *"A friend loves at all times"* (Proverbs 17:17).

So much could be written on this matter of friendship, but my purpose here is to simply say that our friends have not only been "stepping stones over rapid and rough waters," not only an oasis in times of a desert drought, not only a mirror to help us see ourselves, but a source of joy, growth, accomplishment, and fulfillment. Freda would be the first to say, outside of family, our friends make up the best of life. And for me, now on this pilgrimage of grief, my friends have made life bearable and having encouraged me in God have been the ray of hope when the days were darkest.

Some of our best and long-time friends are found in the Westside Baptist Church family. Our theme, "Where Friends Become Family," is a reality for us. Their love and grace have seen me through when otherwise I would have faltered and failed. I count these folks as precious gifts from God.

There is no substitute for a church home—a place to belong and a people to whom you belong. The local church is the tangible Body of Christ. It reflects His external purpose, His love, grace, and forgiveness. It is the community of faith where we are helped, encouraged, and find healing. Here is one example:

The day had been long—and difficult. Appointments had been stacked from early till late. The ministry issues, well, challenging—yes, and some heart wrenching, no, heartbreaking. And beneath these emotionally weighty encounters was my own journey of loss and grief. In fact, some of them seemed to spark feelings of my own grief.

It had been that kind of day. When finally finished, I returned to my office study, sat in my chair, and looked at my desk. My eyes fell to what appeared to be a folded letter. My first thought was, Oh no, not another matter laden with demand. *I started to set it aside for the next day. You know, "don't do today what you can put off to tomorrow," kind of thing. But, that doesn't really fit my profile. And there seemed to be an inner prompting to reach for it, open it, read it. I did. The title was simply, "A Paraphrase of Psalm 23," that beloved song that has found its way into the hearts of so many across the centuries. It started, "Gary, I am your shepherd." My eyes blurred. I felt remembered. I felt presence—not so alone, so overwhelmed.*

I read on. "You will never have need of anything that I want for you. If you will trust me, and really allow me to be your shepherd . . . " Well, here it is, just read it:

Psalm 23
Gary,

I am your shepherd.
You will never have need of anything that I want for you
If you will trust me, and really allow me to be
The shepherd of your life.
I will give to you such great peace of mind
That it will be like lying in the cool green grass
of a springtime meadow;
And as you learn to deepen your love and trust,
A quietness will come over your soul,
Like a serene, calm lake.
It will be a time of great refreshment to your inner man,
Thus preparing you to do whatever tasks I set before you;
And do not minimize any task that I give you to do,
As it is for my honor and glory, not yours.

There will be times when, because of my great love for you,
That it will be necessary for me to lead you into great darkness . . .
Darkness that will be so great
that you will feel as though you are standing
At the very edge of life, with death awaiting you below.
But always remember, I am still your shepherd.
In the darkness you may not be able to see me,
But you have my eternal promise
that I will never leave you or forsake you.
If you will continue to trust me,
Even after you have been through a time of darkness,
I will again flood your heart with such peace
That you could even sit down and eat dinner among your enemies.
Your joy will be so great
That it will spill over into the lives of others,
And as your reward
I will give to you all of the really important things in life;
And when you have completed all
that I have planned for you on Earth,
I want you to come up
And live with me
Forever and ever and ever.

"Darkness that will be so great that you will feel as though you are standing at the very edge of life . . ." That's where I have stood. What an exact description—a darkness that envelopes you. There is no ray, not a glimmer of light. No, not depression: the darkness of hurt, of aloneness, of what can never be again—that darkness.

"I am still your shepherd . . . Even after you have been through a time of darkness, I will again flood your heart with such peace . . . Your joy will be so great that it will spill over into the lives of others. And as a reward, I will give you the really important things of life."

I can say this—never in the darkness have I lost the sense of His presence. How else could I have made this journey and share the experience with you. I do see a ray of light, like the sunrise at dawn with its promise of a bright day. And I do have the really "important things in life": family, friends, purpose, and opportunity. And joy—that state of soul that runs deep like the aquifers of water beneath the surface that spills into rivers and lakes—that gift of God. It's there. And in His grace, there has been enough—and there will be increasingly more to spill over into the lives of others, especially those who need it most, who want it most.

One other important thought: I don't know who placed this wonderful paraphrase of the powerful and cherished 23rd Psalm on my desk, but I know what prompted it—love. Out of awareness of my need, this person of mystery reached out to provide some measure of comfort and encouragement. That is the power of community—of love—especially within the Body of Christ, His Church. What a gift, especially in that alone moment; I wept. Then I smiled. I took a deep breath, looked around the office that had so many memories, my eyes settling on a picture of Freda. In the photograph, she had her bright smile and a mischievous look on her face. My smile widened. I offered a prayer of thanksgiving for her and for the one who held out a hand with the words of the "Good Shepherd." It was late, time to go home. And somehow it was easier to go home. Home, where the most important things of life abide—still.

Karl Menninger remarked, "When people learn to give and receive love, they find healing and hope." That is true for me. That is true for all of us.

In the love of my friends, those who have made the choice to stay, I have found healing and hope. Thank you. In loving me you have loved Freda and her family—our family. And that means even more.

A poem, known as Italian Philosophy, says this:

Count your garden by flowers
Never by the leaves that fall.
Count your days by golden hours
Don't remember clouds at all.

Count your nights by stars, not shadows,
Count your life with smiles, not tears.
And with joy on every birthday,
Count your age by friends, not years.

By this philosophy, I am blessed!

Of course the best friend I have is Jesus Christ. In Him I continue to discover what friendship means, and I have learned that He is the source and empowerment of all the best friendships. In our relationship with Him we are known and loved, and we become a part of His loving family. We have security, and we have help for every need. And when our time here is over, we have a home in His presence—forever (see John 14.1-3).

CHAPTER TWENTY-FOUR
Love: the Ultimate Power

"... *love compels us*," stated the apostle (2 Corinthians 5:14). A simple statement, but when love is understood, it becomes a driving force.

Freda and I knew love from the beginning of our relationship, a love within the context of His love. In spite of challenge and failure, love grew and in the end sustained us in the most difficult days. Here are a few things I learned across the years.

True love comes from God. *"God is love"* (1 John 4:8). *"This is how we know what love is: Jesus Christ laid down his life for us. And we ought to lay down our lives for our brothers* [and sisters]" (1 John 3:16). Once this truth comes home to us, that we have intrinsic value and are unconditionally loved, then we know love and can share love. His love marks us, challenges us, and compels us.

The most important word in any language is *love*. The second most important word is *relationship*. All the love we will ever experience comes through relationship. For love to work in our relationships, a change of attitude is required. When we see and accept the fact that we are flawed, yet loved, then we understand others are not perfect either. They need love and grace, as we do, so we can become love dispensers and grace dispensers. Only then can we love as intended.

Lloyd C. Douglas, in one of his novels, described an encounter between Jesus and Zaccheus. Jesus asked Zaccheus, "Why do you want to change your lifestyle?" Zaccheus replied, "Because I see mirrored in your eyes, the face of the Zaccheus I was meant to be."

This is the way He looks at us—not as we are, but as whom we can become. This is love. This is grace. This is the way we are to dispense love and grace. This is loving well and such love will be returned to us.

I learned also that love requires a change of understanding. We think of love as feeling, but love is a choice; the sentiment of love follows the act of love. Love is extending oneself on behalf of another. As we do, positive feelings usually follow. Even if they don't, love has been experienced and shared. Love is most clearly seen through Christ on the Cross extending himself on our behalf. Through His love within us, we can extend ourselves on behalf of others.

Nelson and Virginia Bell were the parents of Ruth Bell Graham, the late wife of Billy Graham. She told of an experience late in the lives of her parents. She stopped by to see them and found her dad on his knees before her mother. He was putting her shoes on her feet because she was unable to do so. Nelson looked up at Ruth and said, "You know, taking care of your mother is the greatest privilege of my life."

As we grow in our understanding and ability to love, we come to see that extending ourselves on behalf of another is a privilege. Why? Because it reflects the heart of God himself.

One other thing became clear to me. In addition to a change of attitude and understanding, there must also be a change of commitment—a commitment from what I want to what others need. Of course, in love relationships, our needs, and at least some of our wants, should be met. But, whether they are or not, love compels us to seek the best interest of the other.

I wish I had known in the beginning of our life together what I know now. Freda seemed to have a much better grasp of love than I did. In fact, I must say it has been through the love of Christ and the experience of her love that love became clear to me. Jim Brickman wrote a song, "The Love of My Life," which says in part:

> You are the air I need to breathe,
> the river of life inside of me.
> You are the half that made me whole,
> you are the anchor of my soul.
> And you are strong when I am weak,
> you are the words when I can't speak.

You never fail to see me through.
That's the love I found in you.

The love I found in her enabled me, in time, to understand the power and beauty of love. Now my hope and prayer is to love well. In the end, that's all that really matters. And love lives on. As another Brickman lyric says:

Never alone.
I'll be in every beat of your heart,
When you face the unknown,
Whenever you fly,
This isn't good-bye.
My love will follow you, stay with you,
You're never alone.

We find when love is experienced, it follows us—to the end of our days. Such is the power of love in marriage, family, among friends, and even in a random act of love to a stranger. I've often thought that an epitaph with the simple statement, "He loved well" or "She loved well," is perhaps the greatest affirmation one can be given. This is a worthy effort for us all.

Let me make this even more personal. I have been asked, "Will you fall in love again?" Scott Peck says, tongue in cheek, that "Falling in love is like falling insane." In some ways, that's true. I think the question is, "Will you marry again?" I don't have an answer to that question, but I will say a few things that will put the question in a broader context.

For one thing, at this writing, I'm not ready for another significant relationship. I'm still too emotionally attached to Freda, and I'm not finished with the work of grief. I have said from the beginning that when loneliness becomes my friend, I may then be ready to consider another relationship. A mistake that can be made is to bring unresolved grief into another relationship, expecting the other person to bring relief from the pain of loss and be the counselor to our grief. That is an unfair burden on

151

the person and the relationship. I don't want to make that mistake. Once I'm back to a healthy emotional place, once I have learned the lessons of grief, once I have become stronger as a person, then another relationship can be honored.

If I fall in love again, I hope to have done all my thinking before then. After it happens, as Peck suggested, thinking is often not clear. There are important matters to be considered first: matters such as values, compatibility, family, ministry, and life goals. Marriage would be no small decision. Marriage never is, but it can be more complex in some circumstances than others. I am under the persuasion that, if it happens, it will be a gift.

I still wear my wedding band. First and foremost because it serves as a symbol of an enduring love, but also as a part of my grief process. When I arrive at the place of acceptable closure, I will remove the ring. In so doing, I will convey healing and hope. But when I do, it will be a part of family. Here is what I mean.

I have already asked my son and daughter to be a part of this occasion. We will gather as a family, then one of them will share a Scripture that reflects the life Freda and I shared and offer a prayer of thanksgiving. The other will share a Scripture that reflects faith and hope for the future and offer a prayer for guidance. Then any member of the family can share thoughts as desired.

There are several reasons for this. First, I believe it's important for family to be a part of my decisions. They always have been. Why would this change now? How I handle my grief and the decisions I make will affect their lives more than anyone else. Love and respect and wisdom would include them.

Second, I hope it will be a part of their own healing process and our healing as a family. I believe intentional engagement of the process is the primary means of healing and continues contribution even while we grieve. This is engagement of one important issue.

Third, markers are important for good transitions. Engagement for marriage is a marker. Marriage itself is a marker. Markers are important. And this marker would indicate gratitude for the past, love in the present, and hope for the future.

There will never be another Freda, never another first love. There is a sense in which "I will never love like this again." But love I intend to do, with her love having given me a greater understanding and capacity to love. In fact, living with Freda always made me feel that I should be more generous with my life. That I hope to be.

One lyric says it, "The fool loses tomorrow by reaching back for yesterday." Well, I won't reach back to try to live there, but I do value the love and life I experienced with Freda and will benefit from the wisdom the journey provided. That, I believe, is an act of love and provides the best possibility for the future.

CHAPTER TWENTY-FIVE
Heaven: the Ultimate Gift

Of course I believe in Heaven. I have often thought of Heaven; over the years have studied about Heaven; but I must say now that Freda is in Heaven, my passion to understand what life is like for her and what it may be like for us once I am there, presses the question for me. Much will remain a mystery about Heaven, but God has made some things clear.

Life is forever—somewhere. This premise is embedded in the consciousness of all people everywhere. That is true for the Australian Aborigine, the Native American peoples, African tribesman, and the sophisticated American. George Barna, researcher, stated, "An overwhelming majority of Americans believe that there is life after death and that Heaven and hell exist." No matter the geographical location, the worldview, or the level of sophistication, there is a sense in the human heart that life is forever. Cyprian said, "When we are born, we are born not only into this world, we are born into eternity. This life is but a stewardship."

As Christians, this is a firm conviction for us all. It is the biblical view; *"Therefore we are always confident and know that as long as we are at home in the body we are away from the Lord. We live by faith, not by sight"* (2 Corinthians 5:6-7). And again, *"For to me, to live is Christ and to die is gain. If I am to go on living in the body, this will mean fruitful labor for me. Yet what shall I choose? I do not know! I am torn between the two: I desire to depart and be with Christ, which is better by far"* (Philippians 1:21-23).

We can be sure of this—life is forever.

We all know that, for the believer, life will continue in a prepared place. Jesus promised, *"Do not let your hearts be troubled. Trust in God; trust also in me. In my Father's house are many rooms; if it were not so, I would have told you. I am going there to prepare a place for you. And if I go and prepare a place for you, I will come back and take you to be with me that you also may be where I am"* (John 14:1-3). He speaks of a literal place and relationships.

155

Although there remain many unanswered questions, John, in his Revelation (6:9-11), indicates that these assurances: When we die, we go to Heaven (9); we will be remembered for our lives on Earth (9); we will express ourselves audibly (10); and we will have strong familial connection with those on Earth (11). The implications of these statements are immense. And while these implications may not be thoroughly clear to us, we can say with the apostle, *"It is far better"* to be with Christ in Heaven. No wonder we are told to *"Set your minds on things above"* (Colossians 3:2). I must confess failure here. Too often, over the years, my focus has been here and now. To focus on Heaven is a corrective, for when we set our focus on Heaven, it not only changes the way we look at the end of this life, but how we live life now. As C.S. Lewis stated, "If you read history, you will find that the Christians who did most in this present world were just those who thought most about the next."

The purpose of this writing is not to provide a thorough explanation of what the Bible says about Heaven. Rather, it is simply a testimony of my conviction that Heaven exists, Heaven becomes our home through faith in Jesus Christ, we go immediately to Heaven when we die, that there will be recognition, on-going relationships, ministry, and adventure in Heaven. That it will be *"far better"* (Philippians 1:23) than anything we can imagine. And this provides accountability for how we live now and a hope for an eternity with Christ himself and the most cherished persons in our lives.

Lachlan is our four-year-old. He was with me one day in the garden. He found the water hose and, in short order, he had made a mud puddle and pretty much had mud from head to toe. After returning to the house, I said to him, "We must wash before going inside. Digi would want us to." He looked at me straight in the eyes and said, "Digi is in Heaven!" I replied, "I know." He then said with curiosity in his eyes, "Is she back?" The clear indication by his tone of voice and body language was that if she's back, let's wash. If not, let's don't!

Well, once in Heaven, it's for good. Thank God! The only

time believers will return is when Christ returns. As the Bible explains,

"Brothers, we do not want you to be ignorant about those who fall asleep, or to grieve like the rest of men, who have no hope. We believe that Jesus died and rose again and so we believe that God will bring with Jesus those who have fallen asleep in him. According to the Lord's own word, we tell you that we who are still alive, who are left till the coming of the Lord, will certainly not precede those who have fallen asleep. For the Lord himself will come down from heaven, with a loud command, with the voice of the archangel and with the trumpet call of God, and the dead in Christ will rise first. After that, we who are still alive and are left will be caught up together with them in the clouds to meet the Lord in the air. And so we will be with the Lord forever. Therefore encourage each other with these words" (1 Thessalonians 4:13-18).

I sorely miss my wife, Freda, and I still struggle to accept that life together in this life is over. But I find great encouragement in knowing she is in a place *"far better"* and that, in some way, in the mysteries of God, she is still involved in the life of her family and awaits us for an eternity together.

I can live with this! And for this! This is our greatest encouragement.

Epilogue

Is this journey over—the grieving done? No, of course not. There is a sense in which it never will be. But life is better now. I am stronger now. How do I know?

Well, for one thing, I am again in St. Augustine, now one year and eight months later. The overwhelming pain I felt when here before, for the most part, has turned into sweet memories. Yes, I pulled out the letters—again. I was reminded of the purity and strength of her love, I was moved by the beauty of first love, and I longed for that which is no more. But I was not overcome. Instead of the fury of a storm, there was the gentle rain.

After I read through the letters the first time (April of last year), I wrote a note to our two children, Christa and John. I tucked it safely away with the letters. After reading the note, I felt a measure of closure. "This is good," I said to myself.

In addition, I finally got the nerve to go to the hotel where we spent part of our honeymoon and ask to see the room. I thought I had prepared myself, but when I began to speak to the registration attendant, my lips quivered and my voice broke. "Is room 126 occupied?" I asked. "Yes," was the reply. "Well, I have what might be an unusual request. Forty years ago, my wife and I spent the second night of our honeymoon in that room. I'm here to visit and I would like to spend five minutes in the room." "Are you sure it wasn't 130? That is our honeymoon suite." "Yes, I'm sure. We couldn't afford it. It was room 126." "It's occupied until tomorrow at 11:00 a.m." "May I come back then?" "Sure." "Will you be here?" "I will."

Across the remainder of the afternoon, the evening, and the next morning, I couldn't get the room off my mind. I visualized every detail I could remember, after forty years. The time arrived for my visit. Tom, the registration clerk, was there. He remembered my request and immediately asked an attendant to take me to the room. The attendant opened the door and left. I know it seems weird but my heartbeat became rapid, my palms sweaty, and my eyes tearing. I breathed deeply and stepped into the room. It was almost exactly as remembered. Images flooded my mind. I was moved with gratitude.

I knelt beside the bed and prayed. "Thank you, Lord, for the gift of her love, her pristine beauty and purity, and her years of steadfast love." I stopped praying out loud—all of the remaining prayer took place in my heart. I found encouragement in the Scripture which came to mind. *"In the same way, the Spirit helps us in our weakness. We do not know what we ought to pray for, but the Spirit himself intercedes for us through groans that words cannot express. And he who searches our hearts knows the mind of the Spirit, because the Spirit intercedes for the saints in accordance with God's will"* (Romans 8:26-27).

I stood, wiped my tears from my face, went to the door, turned for one last look, and left. Back at the office, I thanked Tom. He reached for a handshake. I appreciated his kindness. As I drove away, I paused in front of the room and listened to our song once more, the same that marked the time we fell in love, "This Guy's in Love with You" by Herb Alpert:

You see this guy, this guy's in love with you
Yes I'm in love who looks at you the way I do
When you smile I can tell we know each other very well

How can I show you I'm glad I got to know you 'cause
I've heard some talk they say you think I'm fine
This guy's in love and what I'd do to make you mine
Tell me now what it is so don't let me be the last to know

My hands are shakin'
don't let my heart keep breaking 'cause
I need your love, I want your love
Say you're in love and you'll be my girl, if not I'll just die

Tell me now is it so don't let me be the last to know
My hands are shakin'
don't let my heart keep breaking 'cause
I need your love, I want your love
Say you're in love and you'll be my girl, if not I'll just die

What was true then is true now. "My hands are shakin',

don't let my heart keep breaking 'cause I need your love, I want your love." I'm thankful that after the passing of the years and the challenges of life—that's still true. As I left the parking lot, I knew I was better.

There is another marker that helps me know I'm seeing light at the end of the tunnel.

Early on I identified my enemies, those things that would work against a healthy grief process. Things like allowing the memories of her suffering to crowd out those of life, health, adventure, and good times, like the "Why" question instead of the "What" question, fear, rebound relationships, and a lack of initiative and focus. I carefully guarded against them and at this point can actually see how that worked in my best interest and the interest of others.

Additionally, there were eight questions that I determined from the start needed to be answered:

1. Who am I without Freda?
2. What will it mean to move forward without her?
3. How can loneliness become my teacher and friend?
4. It's been said that "loneliness is the environment in which we do stupid things." Actually, we do stupid things even without the context of loneliness. However, loneliness does increase the inclination. My hope has been to use loneliness as a tool for healing and strength and an opportunity to help others in the midst of their own loneliness.
5. How can I preserve positive memories?
6. How will I know when and if my grief is clouding my thinking?
7. Can I remain as pastor of Westside without her by my side?
8. How can I make my loss gain for myself and others?

At this sitting, for the most part, these questions have been answered.

One of the songs Freda sang was "Beyond the Open Door." The lyrics say:

In the things familiar we find security

Resisting all the changes that days and years can bring,
When God decides to lead you through an open door
Inviting you to walk in realms you've never walked before.

Beyond the open door is a new and fresh anointing,
Hear the Spirit calling you to go.
Walk on through the door for the Lord will go before you
Into a greater power you've never known before.

As I have listened to this song again and again across the last two years, I have been puzzled by the phrase "into a greater power you've never known before." How could I be stronger without Freda than with her; I could not answer that question. I now can. It's not that I'm stronger without her—it's that I am stronger because of her and because grief has done its work of healing and, of course, because of God's grace. As stated earlier by Stephanie Ericsson, "Grief will make a new person out of you—if it doesn't kill you."

I have walked in realms I have never known before—I have experienced a greater power beyond my own. The door to the future is before me. I'm ready, I think. As has been said, "Don't cry because it's over. Smile because it happened." I'm almost there—maybe.

As I do this revision, I'm in the library at the community college where it all started between us. I'm sitting in the same area of the library. While I have wept, at times, as I have read and revised my writing, being here is not so troubling—it just creates a longing to set the clock back. It still puts a feeling in my stomach like the one you feel in a free fall, and that's okay. I know I'm better and on the road to further healing.

I am stronger. After serving my church family for twenty-five years, I shared with them six of the most important things I had learned:

- Prayer is most important. Without it, we're limited to our own ability. With it, we have the ability that God himself empowers.
- Forgiveness is our greatest need. Without it, we have

no hope of health and growth. With it, we have a life of adventure and hope.

• Love is the defining difference. Without it, we have no reason to live. With it, we have every reason to live.

• Passionate people in our lives are a must. Without them we will never do our best. With them, we exceed our own expectations.

• Resolve is non-negotiable. Without it, we always quit too soon. With it, we experience success beyond what we anticipate.

• Dreams come true. Without them, we won't reach very high. With them, we reach beyond our imagination.

Then, at my 30th Anniversary Celebration, one year and ten months after the loss of Freda, I shared another thing I have learned: *A wounded heart is not the same as a broken spirit.* In fact, a wounded heart can lead to more understanding, a greater capacity to love, a deeper compassion, and a brighter hope. And while I am still on pilgrimage in learning the most important things in life, I am stronger.

I mentioned to you in my introduction that I was writing these words while on a plane to South Africa. I stated "This too, will be a part of my pilgrimage." This is what I meant:

• A safari can be a dangerous place. And so is the place of grief.

• Dr. Jim Lynch, in his ground-breaking work *Broken Heart: The Medical Consequences of Loneliness,* makes it clear that the loneliness of grief can result in medical consequences and even lead to death. Yes, grief can harm you. It can kill you.

• I have long wanted to go on an African safari. Now, I'm here. The rugged beauty of the land holds a certain fascination. And even on the first day, we saw one indigenous animal after another, some small and fleeting, others huge and aggressive. The professional hunter and guide observed, "Everything here can kill you." He was speaking metaphorically, but his point was made. It's a dangerous place to be. He informed us that at least one professional hunter is lost each year due to maiming or death by an animal in the wild. This is not hard to believe with twenty-two species of animals on this 16,000-acre spread, including the cape buffalo, known as Black Death. This buffalo is so named because he is powerful, unpredictable, and hostile. "He can take your life even when you think he can't," said the professional hunter.

· There were also the sixteen species of snakes that crawled the dry ground, rugged rock, and thick bush, the most dangerous, the Black Mamba. These snakes can stand six to eight feet high with a body length of ten plus feet. This is why they often strike the chest and above. And when they do—it's done. There is no antidote for the venom. Lore has it that the only thing you can do is to find a shade tree, lie down, and cross your arms so that when you die, you can easily fit into the coffin.

· As we engage a safari, we deal with harsh terrain, unpredictable challenges; we face our fears; we manage the cold or heat; we expend the energy; and we keep our focus. All of this and more is the price for the *moment*.

· Likewise, dealing with the harsh reality of grief, facing our fears, expending the energy, and keeping our focus is all part of the price for the *moment* of growth and change, or experiencing a renewed passion for life and becoming ready to love again.

· But there is another side of the story. A safari provides a unique and wonderful opportunity to see some of the most beautiful and exotic scenes on Earth, to deepen one's experience with nature, as well as to learn about one's self.

· And for those who hunt or do close-up photography, the thrill of the moment is indescribable. It doesn't really matter (except maybe for the fear factor) whether we are trying to slip up on a majestic Kudu that moves with speed and stealth through the bush or facing unexpectedly a Black Death Cape Buffalo that moves with surprise, vengeance, and with the force of a tornado. The physiology is basically the same—breathing becomes rapid, the heart pounds, palms become sweaty, the body tenses with anticipation, and in that moment, we live. We experience a different dimension of the passion of life. Perhaps more importantly, we discover something more about ourselves, about life, about living.

So it is with grief. While dangerous, it provides unequal opportunity to better understand life, yourself, and others. It can become a pilgrimage of love.

I have engaged the hunt—the pain, the fear, the loneliness, the uncertainties—and I am beginning to feel hope and passion in my life again.

The grief process, for me, has become a pilgrimage of love as I have attempted to honor her love and love family and friends well on the journey as they have loved me.

My journey is just that—my journey. But perhaps, in my journey you can find encouragement and strength for your own and can better understand the journey of grief in others and walk with them in a more helpful way. That is my hope and prayer for you.

As I finish this writing, I'm with my family in the Blue Ridge Mountains of Georgia. It is the second anniversary of Freda's homegoing and Thanksgiving week. I'm sitting in a rocker on the porch overlooking the mountain lake with manuscript in hand. The rain falls softly on the tin roof of the cabin; the smell of smoke drifts to the porch from the fireplace inside. The men of the family are engaged in discussion; the women playing musical chairs with the children, while teaching them cooperation. The aroma of chocolate chip cookies in the oven is making my mouth water. And here I sit in the mountains which Freda so loved, with family she held so dear, writing about our life together—which is now over. But it's not really, is it? Her faith, courage, love, and laughter live in her legacy—her life lives in us as ours move on . . .

It is true − *"No one can go back and have a new beginning. But anyone can start now and have a new ending."*

Addendum

The day is January 31, 2012, seven months after writing the manuscript for this book and a few months before its release. A forward step has been taken during these months. Here is that story.

I awakened excited. I would spend time at the Community College where Freda and I fell in love. I was there to think, pray, and hopefully, make some decisions. Arriving on this cool, beautiful morning, I parked in the lot where Freda once borrowed my car to come play tennis with Smoky, a guy who was quite attracted to her.

I made my way to the student union where Freda and I once danced. She was there as President of the Student Body. I was there at her invitation. I sat and remembered so many scenes. I reached for my Bible and read these words, *"I will say, 'Peace be within you.' For the sake of the house of the Lord, our God, I will seek your prosperity"* (Psalm 122:9) and *"as water reflects a face, so a man's heart reflects the man"* (Proverbs 27:19).

As I thought and prayed through the day, I moved from one place on the campus to another—all of them familiar to Freda and me. The sky was clear, the air crisp, the birds singing.

I gradually worked my way through my preferred vision for the next few years. It seems positive and hopeful. I had a settled peace about my direction.

Then, the other big question—the question of another relationship. This question is so hard to address—especially here where I met the love of my life. But here I must, for I must do this with her.

The first decision, my wedding ring. When does it come off? I have continued to wear it as a symbol of love and as a statement to others. Now that the pain of loss is turning into sweet and empowering memories, there is the possibility of another relationship. Perhaps I will remove it on August 21, which would have been our 42nd wedding anniversary. I will invite family, as discussed earlier, to join me. It is still my intention to make decisions with family in mind as this will be a time of transition for them as well.

I don't know, actually, if the Lord has another marriage for me in His plan. In my heart it seems so, but, if not, then I trust His heart. I thought carefully about the traits I would hope for, naming fourteen of them. But, above them all, is a strong faith in Christ. I desire someone who will bring spiritual strength into my life.

Having made these two decisions, I commit then to the Lord who promises, *"Commit to the Lord whatever you do and you will succeed"* (Proverbs 16:3). I, then, choose three places to pray—one in front of the Fine Arts Building where I recognized for the first time my love for Freda. I knelt and offered thanksgiving for the gift of her love and life. The second place was in front of the library. I can still see, in years past, her walking toward me with that bright smile. The final place was under the pines in the center of the campus—a place that represented the future for me.

One other thing is left to be done—ask Freda for her encouragement in these next steps. I went to the parking lot behind the music building where we had met on many occasions. "Freda, I want to know that you feel these decisions I have made today are good decisions." My heart aches. I weep. I looked up and saw her (in my memory) standing at the side of the auditorium where she and I would often meet. She was smiling. That was it—that was her approval—her encouragement—her reassurance. I cried. I don't want to go forward without her, but I will. In God's strength and hers, I will, depending on His love and guidance.

On my way home, I stopped by the gravesite. Her cousin was there. We talked of Freda and her high school days. I ask, already knowing the answer, "Who was she in high school?" His reply, "She was upper echelon, way above the riff raff." I smiled and said, "Yep!"

Home now, I feel tired and a bit drained, but I feel "at" home. And although she is "at home," her love lingers and always will. I look up at the starlit sky. The stars twinkle, the moon is bright and I see her smile. I can take the next step—when the time comes

Insights from Grief

A Summary and Study Guide

1. Expect your world to be turned upside down and inside out. Even when you may see loss coming, you can't really prepare for its impact because you can't see what's coming around the corner. You have an idea of what you lost, but then keep discovering all you have lost. So hindsight would say, know that a shattering of your world is coming. As Scott Peck says, "Life is difficult. This is the great truth, one of the greatest truths—it is a great truth because once we see this truth, we transcend it." I would say, it is an important truth, that when recognized, provides the possibility to transcend it.

2. For grief to do its work of healing and restoration, we must face it. We can't bury grief. If we try to do so, it will work subconsciously and adversely. We must face it in faith and courage if it is to accomplish its task. It is intended to be friend, not foe. We are to grieve, *"not as those who have no hope"* (1 Thessalonians 4:13). Perhaps what has been written in these pages can help you do so.

3. Don't make significant life decisions while in the throes of grief. Grief clouds our thinking like a fog limits our ability to see. Give yourself time for your thinking to clear.

4. Work hard to love well in the midst of your grief. Our feelings are raw, our fears heightened. Our spirit is sensitive. It is easy to be short and even harsh toward those around us. Make a special effort to be loving. And if you have a loved one in grief, understand that he or she will have difficulty managing feelings and compensate.

5. There will be good days and bad. Enjoy the good days and understand the bad days will be less hard and less frequent as time goes by.

6. Dealing with the practical decisions of life like finances, clothing, special occasions, family gatherings, being single again, being the fifth wheel can be difficult. Give

169

yourself time, seek good counsel if needed, and understand that you will find a new normal, a new balance in
your life again.

7. Grief is a crucible. It's a teacher. It will reveal much to
us about ourselves, about life, and about relationships.
Listen carefully to its wisdom. It reveals something about
how we love and our capacity to love.

8. Grief is a stewardship. If we manage it in faith and under
the guidelines of our Lord, it will not only bring us healing, but what we learn we can share with others and
perhaps make their journey more productive.

9. Relationships in life are what count most. Family defines
our quality of life, and those special friends can make the
definitive difference. One thing is for certain: tough times
will reveal the strength of family and who your real friends
are. A church family, which provides an environment of
faith and love and biblical teaching, can be an anchor for
our soul. Nurture your relationships and be grateful for
them. We need one another and never more than when
facing loss.

10. Loneliness can be fierce. Being alone is tough enough.
Being lonely is worse. And loneliness can occur while in
a crowd. I have said from the beginning of my journey,
"When loneliness becomes my friend and being alone is
okay, then I will know grief has done its duty and I will
be better prepared for companionship again." We can
only offer another who we are when we are alone. This is
important because rebound relationships are not usually
fulfilling or lasting.

11. Memories—good memories bring the joy of yesterday
into today. In them we find encouragement, strength,
and wisdom. Make good memories every day and hold
to the best of them when the memories are all you have
to hold to. Capture the appropriate memories and work
to make them into legacy and heritage.

12. Love carries the day, every day. Love is putting the best

interest of others before our own. Love is the antidote for selfishness and a gift and empowerment to another. Love is a commitment, not a feeling. Allow grief to teach you how to love more deeply.

13. There will come a time, if our grief is done well, that we understand what "let go" and "move on" mean. You can't reach it—it has to come to you. When it does, you will know.

14. Heaven, as believers in Jesus Christ, is our final home. We are all in pilgrimage. We are, in a real sense, "strangers in a foreign land." Each of us must go home, and when we do, we will find it *"far better"* (Philippians 1:23). Until then, what we do matters.

15. Finally, when all is said—all has not yet been said. There are so many experiences, nuances, and moments of insight that have not been included in this writing. Things like the experience of the first Christmas, or birthday, or anniversary, or New Year's without your loved one. Each carries its own challenge and opportunity. Each can become a teachable moment.

Remember, grief is a journey—a pilgrimage. There is no quick fix. The Psalmist said, *"Blessed are those whose strength is in you, who have set their hearts on pilgrimage"* (Psalm 84:5). "Pilgrimage" is literally "in whose heart are the highways" (the highways that people took to respond to God's call to Jerusalem). As one translation has it, *"And how blessed all those in whom you live, whose lives become roads you travel; They wind through lonesome valleys, come upon brooks, discover cool springs and pools brimming with rain! God-traveled, these roads curve up the mountain, and at the last turn—Zion! God in full view!"* (Psalm 84:5-7 The Message).

Grief is a road we travel—in the road there are lonesome valleys, mountains, and, at times, cool springs. In the end, though our view of God may have been dim at times, He comes into "full view." We are "blessed" because we have traveled with

Him and now have a deeper understanding of Him, ourselves, and life. "We found our strength in you" and now you have made us strong!

Materials

Additional Resources by the Author

In Celebration of Love, Marriage, and Sex

A contemporary and practical look at how the love song of Solomon can help engaged and married couples bring and maintain a freshness and celebration to their relationships.

Also, audio and video sets are available from the teaching of Dr. Crawford

Song of Solomon, a message series

In Celebration of Love, Marriage, and Sex, a series taught to college students from the book.

Until My Last Breath

A devotional collection written by Freda Crawford

God's Sustaining Hand

A CD of songs and instrumentals

An Expression of Love

A cookbook of favorite recipes from the Freda Crawford collection

Pilgrim

A single audio love song

Until My Last Breath

A single audio mission song

How to Order:

In Celebration of Love, Marriage, and Sex is available at Amazon and through your favorite bookstore.

All other resources are available at www.garycrawfordleadership.com